BiaMaith Good Food Made Simple
by Liam Boland

Copyright © 2015 Liam Boland. All rights reserved.

First paperback edition printed 2015 in Italy.

A catalogue record for this book is available from the National Irish Library.

SOFTBACK ISBN 978-0-9934622-0-7

Published by BiaMaith

Design by Audrey Kane
*audreykanegraphics@gmail.com*

Photography by Michael O'Neill
*monpics@gmail.com*

# BiaMaith
# GOOD FOOD MADE SIMPLE

## BY LIAM BOLAND

Editors: Aine Bonner and Maureen Gill-Emerson

*For Mum...*

# ACKNOWLEDGMENTS

There are so many people I would like to thank for helping me turn my dream of writing a recipe book into a reality. I have some absolutely fantastic suppliers who came on board and went out of their way to support me with this project. They were Behan's Fruit and Veg and Sam's Seafood in Athlone, Derrycamma Farm Rapeseed Oil in Co. Louth and Quarrymount Freerange Meats in Co. Offaly. These producers and suppliers are at the top of their game and I'm so proud to have them associated with the book. The likes of these are what makes Ireland great when it comes to food.

I would also like to thank the Athlone branch of Allens (www.allens.ie) for loaning me a multitude of gorgeous accessories and props for use in the photo shoot. I loved all their products so much that I will be adding them to my wish-list of things to buy in the near future.

I had a fantastic team who I need to thank - a wonderful photographer, Mick O'Neill, our talented graphic designer Audrey Kane, and my patient editors, Maureen Gill-Emerson and Aine Bonner. My kitchen porters were my cousin, Sean Ryan, and Anthony Henehan. Nicole Sendell was my brilliant kitchen assistant, cleaning up after every whirlwind cooking day. Everybody went above and beyond to ensure the book was finished on time. We had so many people tell us that it wasn't possible to achieve what we have achieved but we all really worked hard to finish the book and I'm delighted with the final product. My aunt, Joan, was also a huge help in offering support and advice, as was my good friend, Garbhan.

Finally, I would like to thank my friends and followers on Facebook and those who visit the BiaMaith page every day. None of this would have been possible without your support, so thank you from the bottom of my heart.

# BiaMaith
## THE STORY SO FAR

I can't quite believe I'm here writing an introduction to my very own cook book. This time last year BiaMaith didn't exist, and as I type, nearly 17,000 people follow my Facebook page. Hundreds of thousands of people read my recipes every week and I've got an online community of people that I truly consider to be part of the BiaMaith family. I feel so blessed to have such a great bunch of in-spirational and warm-hearted individuals who take time out of their busy lives to read, comment and share my recipes on a daily basis. I've come from such a dark place over the past 12 months and honestly couldn't have done it without the support of each and every one of you. For those of you who have stumbled upon this book without having seen my page, this is the BiaMaith story so far…

I've been a chef for most of my life. A few years ago, I unfortunately suffered a heart attack and I had to give up working in professional kitchens. I went from travelling all over the world as a chef and restaurant consultant - even working as a chef for ACDC at their gigs in Wembley Stadium - to being unemployed, on the dole and struggling to get out of bed due to depression. BiaMaith was born after I started posting recipes for my friends on Facebook. They were amazed at how I managed to pull together delicious meals on such a tight budget. They'd come over to see me and I always had some grub on the go, despite the fact that I had very little disposable income after paying my rent in Dublin. They wanted to know how it was possible to have such high quality meals, having paid so little for my ingredients. I managed because I would shop the special offers and get the best deals from local suppliers whenever possible. I cook with ingredients that are readily available in supermarkets across the country and I have taken the skills I learned in professional kitchens all over the world and brought them to the home kitchen so that I can cook great food at low prices. My recipes started quickly being shared online and before I knew it, the BiaMaith family was growing and growing. I do everything for the BiaMaith page myself from a 200-year-old cottage in the Midlands. I had to move there after almost becoming homeless due to spiralling rents in the city. I create all my own recipes, I cook them and I take pictures of the dishes with my phone before sharing everything online. It really is a labour of love and I've managed to continue because I know so many people look to the site for inspiration.

Being a fan of the BiaMaith page doesn't necessarily mean that you're on the dole or even that you're struggling to make ends meet. It means that you love great food and that you want to cook healthy and delicious meals for yourself and your family. The recipes are all really easy and quick to make and generally cost less than a fiver. I also make delicious desserts that always prove to be extremely popular. BiaMaith is about giving back instead of taking. I'm so delighted to be able to share my knowledge about cooking with people. I get thousands of messages every single week from people who need advice or guidance in the kitchen. People have told me that they've started eating together as a family, have turned away from relying on takeaways and processed food and are saving money as a result. It's such a great feeling to know that I have helped these people in some little way. And of course there are also plenty of foodies on my page who love experimenting in the kitchen but may be tired of making the same dinners week in, week out. They love coming onto my page and trying new dishes and creating new family favourites.

Creating this book was the natural next step for me on what's been a whirlwind journey that's seen me going from near-homelessness to being interviewed by Ryan Tubridy and featured in national as well as local newspapers. It was a huge challenge and, more than once, we wondered if we'd manage to pull it off. Apart from a few generous sponsors who provided some of the ingredients for the recipes, I bought everything for the book with money from my dole. A few days during the photoshoot, the electricity in my cottage cut out so I had to cook by candlelight on my gas hob. On top of this, the poor drainage system caused my sink to flood the kitchen a few times. It was hugely frustrating, exhausting and soul-destroying at times. But we got through it. And here we are, just about to send it off to the printers so that you can add a BiaMaith cookbook to your kitchen shelves. I am so proud and ecstatic. Thank you for sharing this journey with me.

# SOUP

| | |
|---|---|
| Mushroom and Sweet Pepper Soup | 28 |
| Irish Brown Bread | 29 |
| Smoked Bacon and Cheddar Cheese Soup | 30-31 |
| Minestrone Soup | 30 |
| Roasted Root Vegetable and Thyme Soup | 32 |
| Chicken and Sweetcorn Soup | 33 |
| Cheese and Onion White Soda Bread | 33 |
| Seafood Chowder | 34-35 |

# LIGHT BITES

| | |
|---|---|
| Bruschetta | 42-43 |
| Garlic and Blue Cheese Mushrooms | 44-45 |
| Easy Caesar Salad | 46-47 |
| Frittata | 48-49 |
| Quiche | 50-51 |

# LAMB

| | |
|---|---|
| Lamb Samosas | 56-57 |
| Slow Cooker Lamb Tajine | 58-59 |
| Minted Lamb Burgers | 60-61 |
| Roast Leg of Irish Lamb | 62-63 |
| Pan-seared Lamb Steaks with Stuffing and Rich Gravy | 64-65 |

# BEEF

| | |
|---|---|
| How to Cook a Steak | 74-75 |
| Steak Sandwich | 76-77 |
| Fillet Steak Sandwich with Goat's Cheese and Cherry Tomato | 78-79 |
| The Perfect Roast Beef and Gravy | 80-81 |
| Slow Cooker BBQ Beef Short Ribs | 82-83 |
| Beef Lasagne | 84-85 |

# CHICKEN

| | |
|---|---|
| Tandoori Roast Chicken | 90-91 |
| Chinese Fried Chicken with Sweet Soy and Chilli | 92 |
| Southern Fried Chicken/Thai Fried Chicken/ Tandoori Fried Chicken | 93 |
| Cajun Chicken Burgers | 94-95 |
| Chicken Cassoulet | 96-97 |
| Healthy Chicken and Pasta Bake | 98-99 |
| Kung Po Chicken | 100 |
| Sweet and Sour Chicken in Crispy Batter | 101 |
| Thai Green Curry | 102-103 |
| The Perfect Roast Chicken | 104-105 |

# PORK

| | |
|---|---|
| Smoked Rasher Spread | 79 |
| Rustic Italian Smoked Ham Stew | 112-113 |
| Pork Fillet Medallions, Creamy Mash and Mushroom Sauce | 114-115 |
| Pork and Apple Burgers | 116 |
| Boiled Bacon and Cabbage | 118-119 |
| Bacon and Cabbage Pie | 120-121 |
| Char Sui Pork Belly | 122-123 |
| Bacon and Mushroom Pasta | 124-125 |
| Spaghetti Amatriciana | 126 |
| Bangers and Mash with Onion Gravy | 127 |

# TURKEY

| | |
|---|---|
| Christmas Roast Turkey | 134-135 |
| No Hassle Turkey and Ham | 136-137 |
| Turkey Leftovers - Bake | 138-139 |
| Turkey Leftovers - Noodles | 140-141 |
| Turkey Burgers | 142-143 |

# FISH

Crab Sandwich Spread 79
Thai Garlic and Chilli Prawns 156-157
Seafood Lasagne 158-159
Herb Crusted Salmon 160-161
Hake Fillet with Warm Salad of Cherry
Tomatoes, Basil and Chorizo 162
Sweet and Sour Prawns in Crispy Batter 163
Seafood Pasta 164
How to Make Basic Pasta 164
Smoked Salmon Pasta 165

# VEGETARIAN

Minted Couscous with Chickpeas and Roasted
Tomatoes 59
Vegetarian Portobello Mushroom Burgers 117
Penne Arrabiata 172-173
Vegan Veggie Lasagne 174-175
Fusilli with Roasted Pepper and Chilli Relish 176-177

# SIDE DISHES

Pilau Rice — 91
How to Cook Broccoli — 182-183
The Perfect Mash (variations) — 184-185
Gratin Potatoes — 186
Mushroom and Shallot Ragout — 187
Green Vegetables with Red Pepper and Basil Butter — 188-189
Giant Onion Rings — 189
Honey and Rosemary Roasted Carrots and Parsnips — 190-191
Sautéed Cabbage with Smoked Bacon and Onion — 192-193
Cauliflower Cheese — 194
Garlic Potatoes — 195
Sage and Onion Stuffing — 196
French Beans with Crispy Bacon and Wholegrain Mustard — 197
Creamy Turnip — 197

# SAUCES - DIPS

Hummus (variations) — 204-205
Roasted Red Pepper and Chilli Relish — 206-207
Napoletana Sauce — 208-209
Hollandaise Sauce (variations) — 210-211
Black Olive Tapenade — 211
Aioli Sauce — 212-213
Tomato Relish — 213
Pepper Sauce — 214
Mushroom and Sweet Pepper Sauce — 214
Mushroom Sauce — 214
Ham Glaze — 215
Béchamel Sauce (variations) — 216-217
Butter (variations) — 218-219
Onion Marmalade — 219

# DESERTS

Maple and Chocolate Tart with Caramelised
Hazelnuts                                      230-231
Apple Crumble                                  232-233
Pecan Pavlova                                  234-235
Chocolate Custard                              235
Poached Pears, Raspberry and
and Mint Coulis with Honey Yoghurt             236-237
Apple Sponge                                   238-239

# CHARTS - GUIDES

Oven Temperatures and Conversions              250-251
Essential Stock Cupboard Ingredients           252-255
Liam's Top Tips on how to Reduce
the Cost of your Weekly Shopping Bill          256-257
Weekly Meal Planner                            258
Calendar of Availability for Fruit
and Vegetables                                 259
Weekly Shopping List                           260-261

SOUPS

■ All the delicious fruit, vegetables and salad ingredients for the book came from Behan's Fruit and Veg in Athlone, Co. Westmeath. It's a really well-known family business and has been supplying fruit and vegetables in the area for the past 27 years. It's my go-to place when creating recipes and I love going in there to buy stuff that I know has been recently picked from the ground by a local farmer. You can't beat that.

Phil and Betty Behan and their daughter Sharon run the business alongside some really friendly staff.

What I love about Behan's is that they source as much as possible locally and then hand pick the rest from the Dublin markets.

Sharon's husband, Ronan, has opened his cheesemonger shop, the Cheese Market, in the same complex. And as followers of my page know, I'm a huge cheese lover so I find it hard to pass his door! Shopping locally is really important to me, and buying loose vegetables and fruits is also a good way of reducing waste and keeping your food bills down.

# BEHAN'S FRUIT AND VEG
## ATHLONE CO WESTMEATH

Phone 090 647 5656 www.behansfruitandveg.com

# MUSHROOM AND SWEET PEPPER SOUP

### Prep time 15 mins •
### Cook time 20 mins • Serves 6-8

## INGREDIENTS

- 3 mixed peppers
- 1 onion
- 300g mushrooms
- 3 vegetable stock cubes
- Black pepper mill
- 1 litre water
  Gluten-free method
- 4 large potatoes
  Gluten method
- 75g flour
- 75g butter or margarine

## METHOD

**1.** Chop the onion, peppers and garlic into small cubes then add to the pot. (Chop and add the potatoes too if you're making the gluten-free version)

**2.** Add 1 litre of water and bring to the boil.

**3.** When boiling, turn down to a simmer and add the sliced mushrooms and stock cubes.

**4.** Cook uncovered for 10 minutes.

**5.** Remove the butter from its foil and place in a small bowl and melt in the microwave.

**6.** Add the flour to the butter and mix to form a smooth paste or roux. Add half of this to the soup with a few twists of the pepper mill. Add the cream and blend with the stick blender. Let it cook for about 5 minutes then add more roux if it isn't thick enough. (Keep this step out if making the gluten-free version)

**7.** Simmer for 5 minutes more, then taste to check the seasoning. Add more salt and pepper if necessary.

■ *Serve with delicious Irish Brown Bread.*

# IRISH BROWN BREAD

Prep time 5 mins •
Cook time 45 mins •
Makes one loaf

## INGREDIENTS
- 350g wholemeal flour
- 125g plain flour
- 325ml buttermilk
- 1½ tsp bread soda
- Pinch of salt

## METHOD
**1.** Pre-heat your oven to 180°C or gas mark 4.
**2.** Sieve the plain flour and bread soda into a bowl, then add the whole-meal flour. Mix really well.
**3.** Add the buttermilk and mix really well again. Pour into a greased loaf tin and bake in the oven for around 45 minutes.
**4.** When cooked, wrap in a clean tea towel and leave to cool.

### Liam's Tip
*You can tell the bread is cooked when you hear a hollow sound when tapping the bottom of the loaf.*

# SMOKED BACON AND CHEDDAR CHEESE SOUP

Anyone who knows me knows of my love for all things cheese. I created this recipe a few years back when I had some extra cheese in the fridge. It's ended up being one of my personal favourites. I adore it with Irish brown bread.

**Prep time 10 mins • Cook time 25 mins • Serves 4-6**

## INGREDIENTS
- **300g cheddar cheese, grated**
- **250g smoked bacon lardons or rashers**
- **2 onions, chopped**
- **1 or 2 chicken stock cubes**
- **30g flour**
- **30g butter or margarine**
- **Bunch of fresh parsley**
- **1 litre water**
- **200ml fresh cream or**
- **100g crème fraiche**
- **Freshly ground black pepper to taste**
- **1 tbsp olive oil**

*Liam's Tip*

*To make it gluten free, mix 4 tbsp of cornflour with 1 tbsp of water to form a paste and use instead of the roux.*

## METHOD
1. Add 1 tbsp of oil to a pot and place on heat.
2. Add the smoked bacon lardons or chopped rashers, chopped onion and chopped garlic. Cook for about 3 minutes.
3. Add the water and 1 stock cube, then stir and leave to simmer for 10 minutes.
4. Melt the butter in a small pot then add the flour. Stir and allow to cook on a low heat for about 2 minutes to form a roux, which is thick and creamy in consistency.
5. Add the roux to the soup, then add the cheese and blend with a stick blender.
6. Chop the parsley and add this along with the pepper, cream or crème fraiche, then stir, taste and adjust seasoning, if necessary. You may need to add the other stock cube depending on how salty the lardons or rashers were.

■ *Serve with delicious Irish Brown Bread (see page 29 for recipe).*

# MINESTRONE SOUP

This is an awesome soup. It's extremely healthy, it tastes delicious and is a firm favourite with kids. It's super quick to make and not expensive either - perfect all around.

*Liam's Tip*

*Feel free to vary the vegetables to suit you and your family's tastes.*

**Prep time 15 mins • Cook time 20 mins • Serves 4-6**

## NGREDIENTS
- **1 x 400g tin chopped tomatoes**
- **2 garlic cloves, finely chopped**
- **1 courgette**
- **1 carrot**
- **1 long stick of celery**
- **1 x 400g tin white butter beans**
- **200g macaroni pasta or penne or broken spaghetti**
- **2 vegetable or chicken stock cubes**
- **Bunch of fresh basil**
- **1 tsp dried oregano**
- **Salt and freshly ground black pepper to taste**
- **1 litre water**

## METHOD
1. Dice all the vegetables into small pieces about half the size of a 1 cent piece.
2. Place the water in a large pot and add the vegetables, chopped tomatoes, stock cubes and pepper.
3. Simmer for 10 minutes, then add the pasta and butter beans and simmer until the pasta is cooked.
4. Chop the basil leaves and mix into the soup.
5. Taste, adjust seasoning if required and serve.

# ROASTED ROOT VEGETABLE AND THYME SOUP *(Gluten free)*

This is a great soup to warm up your bones on a cold winter's day. It's slightly sweet, so kids love it too. You can make extra and freeze it but if you plan on doing this, keep the cream out until you defrost and reheat it.

**Prep time 25 mins • Cook time 25 mins • Serves 4-6**

## INGREDIENTS
- 4 large carrots
- ¼ turnip
- 2 parsnips
- 1 onion
- 200ml fresh cream
- 4 tbsp olive oil
- 4 medium sized potatoes, peeled and chopped
- 3 vegetable stock cubes
- ½ tsp freshly ground black pepper
- Handful of fresh thyme, stalks removed
- 1 litre water

## METHOD
**1.** Pre-heat your oven to 180°C or gas mark 4.
**2.** Peel all the vegetables and cut into fairly large chunks.
**3.** Place in a roasting tin, add 2 tbsp of olive oil and mix to ensure all the vegetables are coated. Roast for 15 minutes.
**4.** Remove the vegetables from the oven and place in a large pot, then add the water, pepper, stock cubes and thyme. Bring to the boil, then simmer for 10 minutes.
**5.** Blend with a stick blender until smooth, then add the cream and blend again to mix.
**6.** You can serve it immediately, but I like to leave it simmering for another 30 minutes.

# CHEESE AND ONION WHITE SODA BREAD

Try this with my Onion Marmalade (see page 219) and experiment with other types of cheese, such as Cashel Blue. Because of the onion and cheese, the bread will be heavy, especially when just out of the oven.

**Prep time 15 mins •
Cook time 45 mins • Makes 1 loaf**

## INGREDIENTS
- 550g self-raising flour
- 2 tsp bread soda
- 250ml buttermilk
- 1 onion, finely sliced
- 250g white cheddar cheese, grated
- 1 tsp salt
- Freshly ground black pepper
  Topping
- Pumpkin seeds
- Mustard seeds

## METHOD
1. Pre-heat your oven to 180°C or gas mark 4.
2. Sieve the flour and bread soda into a large bowl. Mix in the onions, cheese and salt, then add the buttermilk and mix really well.
3. Grease a pan or loaf tin with margarine or butter then add your mixture. Top with mustard seeds and pumpkin seeds, pressing down slightly to hold them in place.
4. Place in your oven for 45 minutes, tap the bottom and if it sounds hollow the bread is ready. Remove from the tin, wrap in a tea towel and allow to cool.

# CHICKEN AND SWEETCORN SOUP

If you don't have much time to cook, then this is the soup for you. You'll throw it together in less than 15 minutes.

**Prep time 5 mins • Cook time 10 mins • Serves 2-4**

## INGREDIENTS
- 2 chicken breasts
- 1 onion, finely chopped
- 1 garlic clove, finely chopped
- 100g sweetcorn
- 4 tbsp cornflour
- 1 chicken stock cube
- Pinch of salt and white pepper to taste
- 600ml water

## METHOD
1. Dice the chicken up into really small pieces. Ensure you use a separate chopping board and thoroughly wash your hands after touching raw chicken.
2. Add the water to a pot, then add the onion, garlic, chicken and sweetcorn.
3. Mix the cornflour with 1 tbsp of cold water to form a paste, then add this along with the stock cube to the soup.
4. Simmer for 10 minutes and season with a pinch of salt and white pepper before serving.

# SEAFOOD CHOWDER

## (Gluten free)

**Prep time 5 mins • Cook time 10 mins • Serves 2**

## INGREDIENTS

- 250g mixed seafood
- ½ tin chopped tomatoes
- 1 medium carrot, peeled and finely diced
- 1 medium potato, peeled and finely diced
- 1 garlic clove, finely chopped
- ¼ tsp freshly ground black pepper
- 1 fish stock cube
- 250ml cream
- 40ml water
- A few sprigs of fresh parsley, chopped
- 2 tbsp oil

## METHOD

**1.** Heat a small drop of good quality oil to a pot and add the diced vegetables. Cook for 2 minutes.

**2.** Add the cream and chopped tomatoes. Cook for 2 minutes to reduce a little and to allow the flavours to infuse.

**3.** Add the stock cube, pepper and chopped parsley, then the seafood mix and water. Cook for 3-4 minutes, or about 5 minutes longer if you prefer the vegetables softer and with less of a bite. Adjust seasoning and serve with crusty rolls or my delicious Irish Brown Bread.

■ *(See page 29 for recipe).*

# Recipe notes

*Recipe notes*

LIGHT
BITES

# BRUSCHETTA

**Prep time 15 mins •**
**Serves 2-4**

## INGREDIENTS
- 2 ciabatta
- 10–15 cherry tomatoes, halved
- ½ red onion, finely chopped
- 1 small garlic clove, finely chopped
- 10 fresh basil leaves
- 2 tbsp olive oil
- ¼ tsp freshly ground black pepper
- 4 tbsp Roasted Red Pepper and Chilli Relish, or 4 tbsp Black Olive Tapenade (see sauces page 200-223), or 4 tbsp basil pesto, or a little of each.

## METHOD
**1.** Add the tomatoes, onion, garlic, basil leaves, olive oil and pepper to a bowl. Mix gently and set to one side.
**2.** Cut the ciabatta in half like you would a burger bun or bap. Cut each slice from corner to corner diagonally so you are left with long triangles.
**3.** Spread your choice of relish or pesto on top then top this with a good spoonful of the tomato mix. Sprinkle with freshly ground pepper and a drizzle of olive oil and serve.

# GARLIC AND BLUE CHEESE MUSHROOMS

This has always been one of my favourite dishes. It's my take on garlic mushrooms and it's always proven to be really popular whenever I've had it on menus over the years. You could also leave the cheese out for a creamy garlic mushroom sauce that's great with pasta, mash or rice. For a gluten-free version, use cornflower mixed with a drop of water instead of the roux. For a lactose-free version, use water instead of milk.

**Prep time 10 mins •
Cook time 20 mins • Serves 2-4**

## INGREDIENTS
- **450g button mushrooms**
- **500ml milk**
- **50g flour**
- **50g butter or margarine**
- **4 garlic cloves, chopped**
- **100g blue cheese**
- **½ vegetable stock cube**
- **Small bunch of chopped parsley**

## METHOD
**1.** Place the milk in a saucepan and put on the heat. When nearly boiled turn it down to a simmer.
**2.** Add the stock cube, garlic and blue cheese. Stir until the cheese melts.
**3.** Place the butter in a cup or bowl and melt in the microwave. Mix in the flour to form a paste. This is a simple roux. You can do it in a pot for a proper roux. Add half of this to the milk and whisk.
**4.** Add the mushrooms and simmer for 15 minutes. It should be thick like a soup. If not, then add more stock. Garnish with parsley on top.
■ *Serve with crusty bread as a starter or over mash for a vegetarian main.*

# EASY CAESAR SALAD

Caesar salad is easily the most popular salad in restaurants all over the world. It's simple, quick and economical to make at home, too. The dressing would normally have anchovies through it but they are expensive and can be hard to find. This recipe will show you how to make a delicious salad without going to the trouble or expense of buying them.

**Prep time 15 mins** •
**Cook time 5 minutes** • **Serves 4**

## INGREDIENTS

- 2 heads of cos lettuce
- 50g fresh parmesan cheese, grated
- 6 tbsp mayonnaise
- 2 garlic cloves, chopped
- Small bunch of parsley, chopped
- 3 slices of bread
- 4 tbsp olive oil
- Freshly ground black pepper

## METHOD

**1.** Wash the lettuce leaves and set to one side to drain.
**2.** Cut the crusts off the bread and cut into 4 strips then cut into 4 more which will leave you with little squares.
**3.** Heat the olive oil in a pan, drop a piece of bread in to test if it's hot enough. It should start to sizzle slightly straight away. Add the bread so that one side is facing down.
**4.** Cook for about 30 seconds then turn each one over and cook for another 20 seconds. Remove from the pan and place on a plate lined with kitchen paper to soak up any excess oil.
**5.** Add the mayonnaise to a cup then add the chopped parsley and garlic followed by a hint of freshly ground black pepper and 2 tbsp of water. Mix really well until smooth.
**6.** Place the lettuce leaves in a big bowl then add as much or little of the dressing to suit your tastes. Mix well then place the dressed leaves in serving bowls.
**7.** Dot the croutons around the top then sprinkle with grated parmesan followed by a hint of freshly ground black pepper.

## Liam's tip

Season a breast
of chicken with olive oil,
salt, black pepper, garlic and
paprika. Pan fry this until cooked
through. Slice and serve over the
salad to make it a chicken
Caesar salad.

# FRITTATA

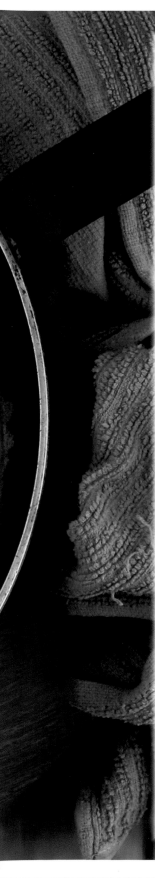

## BASIC FRITTATA

Frittata is an Italian dish made from eggs and is similar to an omelette. The main difference, however, is that a frittata is more airy and is not folded like an omelette. Instead it is finished under a hot grill or turned over.

**Prep time 10mins •
Cook time 10 mins • Serves 4-6**

### INGREDIENTS
- 6 large eggs
- 100ml cream or crème fraiche
- 2 medium onions, thinly sliced
- 2 garlic cloves, chopped
- Bunch of fresh parsley
- 15–20 basil leaves
- Good pinch of freshly ground pepper
- 30g fresh parmesan cheese, grated
- 3 tbsp olive oil

### METHOD
**1.** Pre-heat your grill to just above medium. Place a shelf at a level that will leave a two inch gap between the top of the pan and the grill.
**2.** Break the eggs into a bowl then add the salt, pepper, basil and parmesan. Mix really well with a whisk then add the cream or crème fraiche and whisk well once more.
**3.** Heat the oil in a non-stick pan over a medium heat on the hob.
**4.** Add the garlic and onions and cook for 1 minute.
**5.** Pour in the eggs and whisk well then allow them to settle so they coat the entire base of the pan.
**6.** Turn the heat down to just below medium and leave to cook for about 5 minutes.
**7.** Remove from the hob and place the pan under the grill and leave for 5 minutes, until the top starts to brown.
**8.** Remove the pan from under the grill and place a plate on top of it. Slowly flip the pan over so the frittata drops onto the plate. Cover the frittata with another plate and flip them over so that the frittata is facing the right way up, ready to cut.

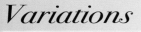

## *Variations*

### ■ GOAT'S CHEESE AND CHERRY TOMATO FRITTATA

#### INGREDIENTS
- 10 cherry tomatoes
- 120g goat's cheese, sliced

#### METHOD
**1.** Follow the basic recipe and add the cherry tomatoes when you add the eggs to the pan.
**2.** Just before you place the frittata under the grill, gently pop the goat's cheese on top and continue with the method in the basic recipe.

### ■ ROASTED VEGETABLE AND OLIVE FRITTATA

#### INGREDIENTS
- ½ aubergine
- 1 courgette
- 2 peppers
- 6 cherry tomatoes or 6 sundried tomatoes
- 12 black or green olives, stones removed
- pinch of salt and freshly ground black pepper

#### METHOD
**1.** Cut the aubergine, courgette and peppers into 2cm slices.
**2.** Drizzle with olive oil and a hint of salt and pepper and grill for 4 minutes on each side.
**3.** Add the vegetables and tomatoes just before you stop mixing the eggs during step 5 of the basic recipe.
**4.** Dot the olives around the top of the frittata before placing under the grill and continuing with the basic recipe.

# QUICHE

Quiche is great in so many ways. I love it cold on a summer's day, either for picnics or lunch, or in the evening with a salad. I also like it served alongside a platter of cheese and cold meats with some nice relishes. It is one of those dishes that can cost very little to make, so if you are on a tight budget it's a great midweek dinner served with peas and homemade chips.

**Prep time 1-2 hours • Cook time 30-45 mins • Serves 4-6**

## INGREDIENTS

**For the pastry**
- **250g plain flour**
- **125g butter or margarine**
- **1 egg**
- **2 tsp cold water**

**For the filling**
- **6 eggs**
- **50g Greek yoghurt**
- **50ml cream**
- **Pinch of salt and pepper to taste**

## METHOD

**1.** Add the flour and salt to a bowl then, using the tips of your fingers, rub the butter into the flour until you are left with a fine sand-like crumb.

**2.** Add the egg and mix in using a cold, metal spoon or the flat side of a knife. If it needs more liquid, add the water.

**3.** When it forms a dough, wrap it in cling film then place in the fridge for 1–2 hours. When ready, remove the pastry from the fridge and pre-heat your oven to 180°C or gas mark 4.

**4.** Cut the dough in two even pieces. Roll one out a little larger than a 23cm quiche dish. Gently and loosely fold the pastry and place it over the dish, then unfold it so it covers the whole dish. Press the dough into the edges lightly. Allow it to sit for a minute or two then trim around the edges using a knife.

**5.** Pierce 4 or 5 holes around the base with a fork to stop the pastry rising.

**6.** Blind bake this for 15 minutes by covering the top with baking parchment, then hold this down in place with raw rice or blind baking beads. This stops the pastry from rising while baking.

**7.** When baked, remove from the oven then remove the baking parchment and rice or beads.

**8.** Beat the eggs in a bowl then add the cream, Greek yoghurt, salt and pepper. Beat these really well with a whisk.

**9.** Pour the egg mix into the pastry case and return to the oven for 15-20 minutes.

## *Variations*

### ■ ROASTED ITALIAN VEGETABLE

#### INGREDIENTS
- 1 courgette, sliced
- 2 peppers
- ½ aubergine, sliced
- ½ red onion
- 1 garlic clove, chopped
- 8-10 cherry tomatoes
- 4 tbsp olive oil
- Salt and freshly ground black pepper

#### METHOD
**1.** Coat the peppers in half of the olive oil and roast for 15-20 minutes on each side.
**2.** Mix the garlic with the remaining olive oil, salt and pepper and coat the remaining vegetables. Roast on a baking tray for 10-15 minutes.

**3.** Continue with the basic recipe and after the pastry is blind baked, line it with the roasted vegetables.
**4.** Pour the egg mix over the vegetables and cook for 20-25 minutes.

### ■ HAM AND CHEESE

#### INGREDIENTS
- 200g sliced ham, cooked bacon or rashers
- 150g cheddar cheese, grated

#### METHOD
**1.** Add the ham and cheese when whisking the eggs then follow the basic recipe.

### ■ TOMATO & BASIL

#### INGREDIENTS
- 6-8 tomatoes
- 20 fresh basil leaves
- 1 red onion

#### METHOD
**1.** Cut the tomatoes into chunks, slice the onions and tear apart the basil leaves.
**2.** Add these to the egg mix and stir, then follow the basic recipe.

### ■ 3 CHEESE QUICHE

#### INGREDIENTS
- 100g white cheddar
- 100g brie
- 100g Gouda, or similar hard cheese

#### METHOD
**1.** Grate the cheddar and the hard cheese and break the brie into small chunks.
**2.** Add them to the egg mix and stir, then follow the basic recipe.

# Recipe notes

LAMB

# LAMB SAMOSAS

These aren't like the samosas you'd get in most Indian restaurants as many use packaged pastry. However, they are exactly like you would get on the streets of Mumbai. They are a little dry if eaten on their own but amazing with the dip. If you don't like mint, use a little chilli, coriander and lime juice instead. These were made by my kitchen assistant, Nicole, who was a fantastic help while I was working on the book.

**Prep time 1 hour 25 mins •**
**Cook time 30 mins • Serves 6-8**

## INGREDIENTS
**The pastry**
- **150g plain flour**
- **115g butter or margarine**
- **1 tsp turmeric**
- **1 tsp curry powder (I used medium)**
- **1 tsp salt**
- **1 egg**
  **The filling**
- **250g minced lamb**
- **1 tsp ground cumin**
- **1 garlic clove, chopped**
- **Small handful of fresh coriander**
- **1 slice of red pepper, finely chopped**
- **½ onion, finely chopped**
- **1 tbsp olive oil**
  **The dip**
- **100g Greek yoghurt**
- **15-20 fresh mint leaves**

## METHOD
**1.** Sieve the flour into a medium-sized bowl, then add the spices and mix well.
**2.** Add the butter, using only the tips of your fingers. If you use your whole hand the pastry will warm up too much and become stretchy.
**3.** Add the egg and mix in using a metal spoon or knife. Continue mixing until you are left with a smooth dough. Wrap this in cling film or foil and leave in the fridge for at least 1 hour.

**4.** While the dough is resting, heat 1 tbsp of oil in a pan and fry the onion, garlic and mince. Add the rest of the ingredients and cook until the mince has browned. It will be slightly dry to taste but that's how it should be. Set aside to cool.
**5.** At this point, make the dip by simply chopping the mint and mixing it with the yogurt. Set aside.
**6.** Pre-heat your oven to 180°C or gas mark 4 at this point.
**7.** Remove the dough from the fridge and cut into 6 even pieces. Roll each piece out into a circle about the size of a saucer. You could use a saucer to cut out the shapes if you find this easier. The pieces will be nice and thin.
**8.** Put a spoonful of the lamb mix in the center of each circle, then brush all around the edges with a beaten egg.
**9.** Fold the pastry in half to form a half moon shape then pierce two fork holes in the top. Do this with each one, then place on a baking tray lined with grease-proof paper.
**10.** Brush the top with a beaten egg and bake for 15–20 minutes. The pastry should be firm to the touch.

■ *Serve with a nice salad and the mint dip you made earlier.*

# SLOW COOKER LAMB TAJINE

Prep time 10 mins •
Cook time 6-8 hours •
Serves 4-6

## INGREDIENTS

- 450g diced lamb (you can use beef pieces if you prefer)
- 1 tsp ground cumin
- 1 tsp ground cinnamon or a small cinnamon stick
- 1 tsp turmeric
- 1 tsp smoked paprika
- ½ tsp freshly ground black pepper
- 3 carrots, peeled and cut into batons (long thin rectangles)
- 1 onion, chopped
- 4 garlic cloves, chopped
- 10 dates, stones removed

*Unlike I did in the book, don't forget to add . . .*

- **500g Tomato Passata**
- **250ml chicken stock (or 1 chicken stock cube dissolved in 250ml boiling water)**

## METHOD

**1.** Add all the ingredients into a slow cooker or a casserole dish.

**2.** Mix well then cook on low if using a slow cooker, or in a preheated oven at 100°C for 6–8 hours.

**3.** When ready, check the seasoning and adjust if necessary.

■ *Serve with couscous, rice or a few spuds. I love it with mash with a hint of horseradish mixed through*.

# MINTED COUSCOUS WITH CHICKPEAS AND ROASTED TOMATOES

Couscous is one of those things you either love or hate. I belong to the latter group, it's never appealed to me, even when I tried it a few different ways while in Morocco. It is seriously popular though, especially with those who are health conscious. Plus it's very easy to prepare, just add hot water and seasoning, fluff it up with a fork and you're done.

**Prep time 5 mins ●
Cook time 10 mins ● Serves 4**

## INGREDIENTS
- 2 coffee mugs of instant couscous
- 2 of the same mugs filled with boiling water
- 15 fresh mint leaves, chopped
- Pinch of salt
- Pinch of ground cumin
- ½ chicken or veg stock cube
- 15g butter
- 2 tbsp olive oil
- 2 garlic cloves, chopped
- 16 cherry tomatoes
- 1 x 400g tin chickpeas, drained

## METHOD
**1.** Pre-heat your oven to 160°C or gas mark 3.
**2.** Boil the water then dissolve the stock cube in it.
**3.** Place the couscous and chickpeas in a bowl and pour the water over the top. Cover and leave to sit for 10 minutes.
**4.** Mix the garlic with the olive oil, then add the cherry tomatoes and stir. Pop them onto a baking tray and bake for 6 minutes.
**5.** Remove the cover from the couscous - it should have soaked up all the water. Stir well with a fork then add the butter, salt, cumin and chopped mint then stir again.
**6.** Add the tomatoes and give it one more gentle stir before tasting and serving.

### Liam's tip
*Chop half a red chilli then mix it through 50g of Greek yoghurt. Spread this on an iceberg lettuce leaf then pop on a spoonful of the couscous. Roll up and munch away for a light snack.*

# MINTED LAMB BURGER

Lamb and mint always go so well together. They are great in a burger, especially when accompanied with a healthy yoghurt sauce.

**Prep Time 10 mins •**
**Cook Time 15 mins • Serves 4-6**

## INGREDIENTS
- 450g minced lamb
- 10–15 mint leaves
- Pinch of salt and freshly ground pepper
- Oil for frying
- 4–6 burger baps
- 75g Greek yoghurt
- 15 chives or 5 mint leaves
- 1 red onion, sliced
- 2 large tomatoes, sliced
- 2 tbsp olive oil
- Handful of baby spinach leaves or any lettuce leaves you like

## METHOD
**1.** Mix the lamb, mint, salt and pepper in a medium-sized bowl.
**2.** Divide into 4-6 pieces then, using your hands, shape each into a burger. Try to get rid of as much air as possible. The burger should hold together in your hands.
**3.** Heat your grill or a pan. If using the grill, brush the burgers with some oil before cooking. If using a pan, add the oil to the pan and heat.
**4.** Cook the burgers for about 7 minutes on each side in the pan or about 10 minutes if grilling.
**5.** Chop the chives or remaining mint. Put them in a cup, add the Greek yoghurt and mix. Spread some on the bottom buns, then add sliced onions and tomatoes, followed by lettuce leaves and the burger. Top with more sauce and the top of the bun.

### Liam's tip
*If you haven't tried orange, mint and lamb together then you really should. I would serve this with a green salad topped with orange segments and a Greek yoghurt and mint dressing just like the one for the burger but with 1 tsp of water added to thin it down a bit.*

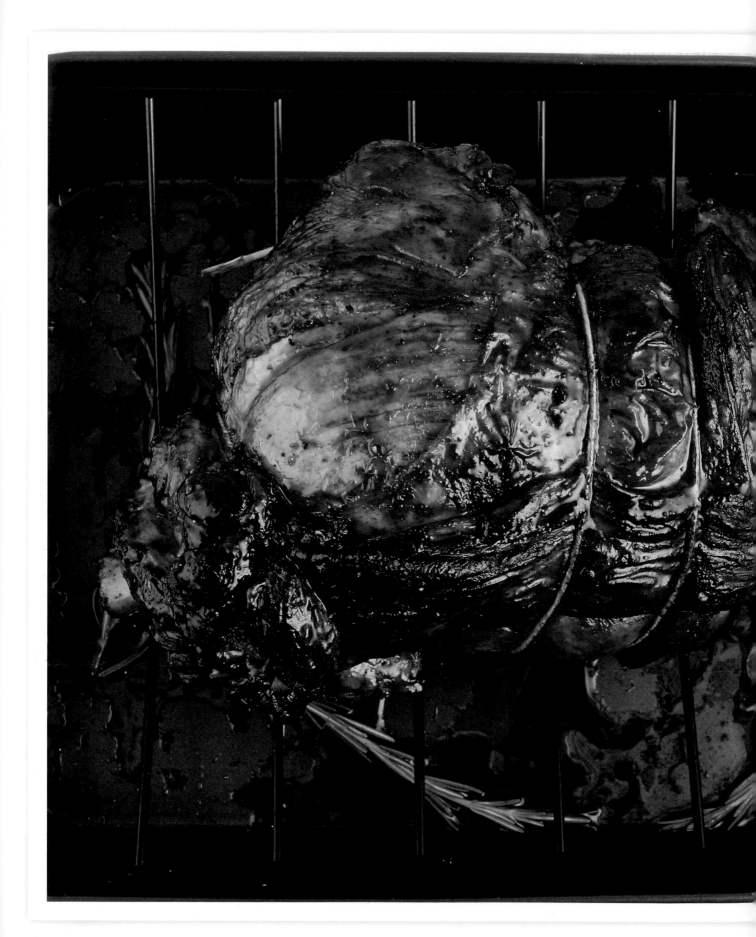

# ROAST LEG OF IRISH LAMB

**Prep time 15 mins** ●
**Cook time 2-2½ hours** ● **Serves 4**

Lamb is amazing when cooked right. It is succulent and bursting with flavour, especially when you follow my cooking method. Roasting a leg of lamb isn't too difficult. The main thing is you don't over cook it or it will end up tough and dry.

## INGREDIENTS

- **1 leg of lamb with the bone left in**
- **6–8 garlic cloves**
- **2 sprigs of fresh rosemary, stalks removed**
- **4 tbsp honey (optional)**
- **2 tbsp paprika**
- **100ml Derrycamma Farm Rapeseed Oil**

## METHOD

1. Pre-heat oven to 200°C or gas mark 6.
2. Pierce the flesh of the lamb with a sharp knife 6-8 times, then push a whole peeled garlic clove in each piercing. Pierce 4 more times and pop some rosemary into these ones.
3. Take a cup or small bowl and pour in some rapeseed oil.
4. Add the paprika and the rest of the rosemary and stir well.
5. Pour this over the meat and rub in well with your hands so that the entire joint is coated.
6. Roast for 30 minutes. Remove from the oven and cover the meat with tin foil then reduce the heat to 180°C or gas mark 4. Return to the oven and cook for a further 1 hr 30 minutes.
7. Remove from the oven and brush the roast with honey then cook uncovered for a further 15-30 minutes, depending on the size of the leg.
8. To check if the lamb is cooked, pierce the flesh with a skewer or sharp knife. If the juices run clear, it is cooked through. Allow the meat to rest for a little while before carving and serving.

## Liam's tip

*Follow the recipe for stuffing on page 196 then carve some slices of lamb. Lay one slice down on a baking tray then top it with a good handful of stuffing. Top that with another slice or two of lamb. Do this for as many portions as you need. Pour over a little gravy and add 25ml of water to the tray. Cover with foil and place in a pre-heated oven at 180°C, gas mark 4 for 10 minutes. Plate up the lamb and top with a little gravy and serve.*

# PAN-SEARED LAMB STEAKS WITH STUFFING AND RICH GRAVY

This dish is so hearty and delicious - it's one of my favourites. It's one of those that you can throw together really quickly but looks and tastes so impressive. If you're cooking for just a couple of people, it's a tasty alternative to a Sunday roast.

**Prep time 10 mins •**
**Cook time 20 mins • Serves 4**

## INGREDIENTS

- **4 lamb leg steaks, about 400g or 12-16 cutlets**
- **Salt and pepper to taste**
- **5 tbsp Derrycamma Farm Rapeseed Oil**
- **Sage and Onion Stuffing from page 196**
  **For the gravy**
- **¼ onion, chopped**
- **¼ clove garlic, finely chopped**
- **20ml red wine**
- **200ml water**
- **¼ tin chopped tomatoes**
- **50g butter or margarine**
- **2 tbsp flour**
- **Gravy granules (optional)**
- **Freshly ground black pepper**

## METHOD

1. Pre-heat your oven to 180°C or gas mark 4.
2. Make Sage and Onion Stuffing.
3. Add the paprika to a bowl and mix with two or three turns of the pepper mill and a generous pinch of salt. Mix this with 4 tbsp of rapeseed oil then dip the steaks in, coating each side.
4. Heat a pan and when it's piping hot, add each steak or cutlet and fry for 30 seconds on each side.
5. Tear off enough tin foil to hold the stuffing and steak. Place the stuffing on the foil then place the steaks on top. Seal the tin foil but leave a tiny gap at the top.
6. Place on an oven proof dish or roasting tin and cook in the oven for 17-20 minutes.
7. Meanwhile, heat 1 tsp of oil in a small pot, then add the onions and garlic and cook on a low heat for 2-3 minutes.
8. Turn up the heat and add the red wine and chopped tomatoes. Reduce for a minute then add 200ml of water. When this boils, you can add gravy granules to thicken.
9. Remove the lamb from the oven.
■ *Serve with gravy and mash.*

# Recipe notes

BEEF

■ All the beef in the book was supplied by Quarrymount Free Range Meats, which is based just outside Tullamore in Co. Offaly and owned by farmer, Ray Dunne.

This meat is just second to none. The roasts were succulent and melt in the mouth and the ribs were one of the most popular dishes that I cooked during the photoshoots.

Ray puts his heart and soul into his products - the attention to detail in how he raises his animals and in how they are butchered, really sets it apart from supermarket meat. The cattle, sheep, chickens and pigs all graze in a natural outdoor environment and the best quality birds and animals are selected for sale. Ray sells his meat - which is traditionally 'dry-aged' - at farmers markets and through a meat box scheme on www.freerangemeats. ie. It's fantastic that you can get these products delivered right to your door.

Apart from the tender and delicious products, what I love about the meat from Quarrymount is that the animals have been reared naturally and well taken care of. You really know what you're getting, which is fantastic.

### FARMERS MARKET
Saturdays: Kilcruttan, Tullamore, Co. Offaly
Marley Park, Dublin and Limerick Milk Market
Sundays: Dun Laoghaire, Dublin Farmleigh House, Phoenix Park, Dublin

# QUARRYMOUNT FREE RANGE MEATS
## TULLAMORE, CO. OFFALY

Phone 086 8331006 or email raydunne@freerangemeats.ie

# HOW TO COOK A STEAK

Are you one of those people who can never cook a steak properly? You aren't the only one. The cooking question I get asked the most is, "how do I cook a steak?" Below you'll find my tips on how to do it properly. Throughout the book you'll find many accompaniments to go with a nice steak. Check out the sauces starting on page 202 or the mashed potatoes on page 184. I particularly recommend the Smoked Bacon and Cheddar Cheese Mash. Pop some mushroom, pepper or béarnaise sauce on the side and serve with some lovely green veggies from page 188 and you will have a feast guaranteed to impress any guest or family member.

### Buying Guide
● Look for meat that has been hung for 21 days. It will taste better and be more tender.
● Avoid dry or grey looking meat as it isn't fresh. Press down on the flesh of the meat with your finger if it is in a packet or ask your butcher to do so if it isn't.
● The best fresh meat should have plenty of give and shouldn't bounce back. If the flesh doesn't give or if it bounces back really quickly, don't buy it as it won't be tender.

### Checking the fat
A marble, or a thin layer of fat through a steak, especially a rib eye steak, is a good sign. This will melt through the meat when cooking and enhance the overall flavour.

### Cooking Tips
● A hot, clean pan is essential. A griddle pan is even better. The ridges on the griddle pan allow hot air to flow under the steak, which cooks it more evenly.
● You should season the steak with oil, salt and pepper before cooking it. Don't oil the pan, oil the steak.
● For a really mouth-watering steak use my special seasoning, which really enhances the flavour of the steak.

### *My special seasoning*
**1.** Mix 1 part paprika, 1 part freshly ground black pepper and 1 part salt to 3 parts Derrycamma Farm Rapeseed Oil.
**2.** Mix these together, then dip the steaks in one at a time.
**3.** Heat your pan until very hot, then pop the steaks down one at a time. It is very important that you don't overload the pan or they will stew rather than fry.
**4.** Get a small knob of butter and add to the pan for the final 2 minutes of cooking time (1 minute for blue steaks).
**5.** Allow the butter to melt, then spoon it over the steaks as they cook. This is known as basting.

**■ Blue**

■ BLUE Cook for about 1-2 minutes on each side. It will be soft to the touch when you press down on it. The flesh will be a deep red, almost purple colour. The internal temperature will be 47–52°C. Only buy blue steak from a butcher you really trust or eat it at a reputable restaurant.

**■ Rare**

■ RARE Cook for 3-4 minutes on each side. It will be soft yet spongy to the touch when you press down on it. The flesh will be bright red and red juices will appear on top when pressed. The internal temperature will be 52–55°C.

**■ Medium**

■ MEDIUM Cook for 5–6 minutes on each side. It will be a little firmer than a rare steak and a mixture of clear and red juices will appear when pressed. The flesh will appear pink. I personally prefer it a little pink like in the picture. I cook mine 5 minutes each side, but cook for 6 minutes each side if you like it done a little more. The internal temperature will be 60–65°C.

**■ Medium Well**

■ MEDIUM WELL If you like a well done steak then this is the one I highly recommend you go for instead. Cook for 7-8 minutes on each side. It will feel firm to the touch and clear juice will still appear on the surface when pressed. The flesh will have a very slight pink line if you cook it for 7 minutes each side. This will disappear and it will be brown right through if you give it the extra time and do it 8 minutes each side. The internal temperature will be 65–69°C.

**■ Well Done**

■ WELL DONE Cook for 9–10 minutes each side. It will be firm to the touch and a small amount of clear juices will rise to the top when pressed. The flesh will be brown with no trace of pink at all. The internal temperature will be 71–100°C.

# STEAK SANDWICH

You'll often find my friends and I tucking into a few of these washed down with a craft beer or two while watching the rugby on the telly. I can prepare everything in advance, enjoy the first half of the game, flash fry the steaks during half time and throw it all together before the second half. To me, a steak sandwich is something you should be able to take a bite out of and not have to eat with a knife and fork. Using really thin minute steak strips means you can, but if you use a sirloin steak you'll need cutlery.

**Prep time 10 mins •**
**Cook time 10 mins • Serves 4**

## INGREDIENTS

- **450g minute steak strips (very thin steak)**
- **1 red pepper, sliced**
- **1 garlic clove, finely chopped**
- **1 red onion, sliced**
- **4-8 lettuce leaves**
- **4 ciabatta or baguettes**
- **16 cherry tomatoes or 4 regular tomatoes**
- **½ tsp salt and freshly ground pepper**
- **2 tbsp Derrycamma Farm Rapeseed Oil**
- **2 tsp paprika**
- **8 tbsp Onion Marmalade (optional - see page 219 for recipe)**
- **8 tbsp Tomato Relish (optional - see page 213 for recipe)**
- **American mustard, a good dollop for each**
- **Mayonnaise, a good dollop for each**

## METHOD

**1.** Place the red pepper, onion and garlic in a bowl. Cut the cherry tomatoes in half, or if using regular tomatoes, chop them, then add to the bowl. Set to one side.

**2.** In a second little bowl, place the rapeseed oil, salt, pepper paprika and mix. Coat the steak in this.

**3.** Halve the ciabatta and leave to one side.

**4.** Heat a griddle or frying pan without oil. Place the coated steaks on the pan, ensuring you don't overfill it or they will stew and end up tough. Fry them for 2 minutes on each side.

**5.** Meanwhile, coat the bottom of the ciabatta with the relish or mayonnaise, place a slice of steak on this then top with some of the tomato, followed by a little more onion marmalade, relish or mayonnaise.

Top this with the lettuce, another piece of steak then the American mustard. Pop the top of the bread on and serve.

# FILLET STEAK SANDWICH WITH GOAT'S CHEESE AND CHERRY TOMATO

I made this for my mate, Dessie Barry, one day and he has been raving about it ever since. It's simple to prepare and tastes amazing. This proves how a few simple ingredients can be delicious when paired together.

**Prep time 10 mins •
Cook time 5 mins • Serves 2-4**

### INGREDIENTS
- 400g fillet steak medallions, cut about 3cm thin
- 4 slices of Irish Brown Soda Bread (see page 29)
- 150g soft goats cheese
- 12 cherry tomatoes, halved
- 1 yellow pepper, sliced
- 1 red onion, thinly sliced
- 12 fresh basil leaves
- 25g butter
- Good handful of mixed lettuce leaves (baby leaves are best)
- Hint of freshly ground black pepper and salt
- 2 tsp paprika
- 1 garlic clove, finely chopped
- 2 tbsp Derrycamma Farm Rapeseed Oil plus a drizzle for the salad topping

### METHOD
**1.** In a bowl, mix the garlic, pepper, salt and paprika with the oil, then dip the steaks in this and set to one side.
**2.** Heat a pan, then cook the steaks for about 2 minutes per side.
**3.** Remove to a plate or chopping board and allow rest for 2-3 minutes.
**4.** Meanwhile, butter the bread, pop some of the lettuce leaves on top then add a steak slice on each.
**5.** Mix the sliced onions, basil, yellow pepper and tomatoes in a bowl.
**6.** Throw in a dash of rapeseed oil and a sprinkling of salt and pepper. Place a handful on top of each sandwich.
**6.** Cut the goat's cheese into cubes and dot these around the top before serving.

# SANDWICH SPREAD

## ■ SMOKED RASHER SPREAD

I love this with cheese and a nice paté, or mixed into a pasta dish. It's even great on boiled spuds or mixed through some mashed turnips or potatoes.

**Prep time 15 mins • Cook time 15 mins • Makes 2 jars**

### INGREDIENTS
- 600g smoked back rashers
- 200g smoked streaky rashers, rind removed
- 2 spring onions
- 2 tsp dark brown demerara sugar
- 1 garlic clove
- 50g real butter
- 1 tbsp honey
- Small bunch parsley

### METHOD
**1.** Pre-heat your oven to 180°C or gas mark 4.
**2.** Wrap all the rashers loosely in tin foil. Seal it as best you can.
**3.** Place it in the oven for 15 minutes, remove and allow to cool down slightly. You don't want the bacon fat to set.
**4.** Add the bacon and all the cooking juices into a food processor with all the other ingredients, then blitz until it starts to form a paste.
**5.** Taste. If it isn't too salty I like to add a little grated parmesan cheese and mix it in well. 50g would do but add a little at a time and taste to ensure you don't make it too salty.
**6.** Allow to cool then place in sterilised jars and store in your fridge for up to 4 days.

## ■ CRAB SANDWICH SPREAD

I seriously love shellfish. It's so delicious. This is a very easy to prepare spread that is ideal to use in pasta dishes or most especially as a sandwich topping or filling. Spread it on toast and have it with cheese. Or spread it on brown bread and top with crispy salad leaves, thick cut tomatoes, spring onions and a light lemon mayonnaise.

**Prep time 10 mins • Serves 2**

### INGREDIENTS
- 200g cooked crab meat
- 25g butter
- 2 spring onions
- 1 small garlic clove
- Small bunch of fresh dill, chive and parsley
- Pinch of salt and freshly ground black pepper
- 2 tsp lemon juice

### METHOD
**1.** Place all the ingredients in a food processor or bowl then blitz on pulse for about 30 seconds.
**2.** Taste, and adjust the seasoning or add more lemon juice if necessary. This will keep in the fridge for 2 days.

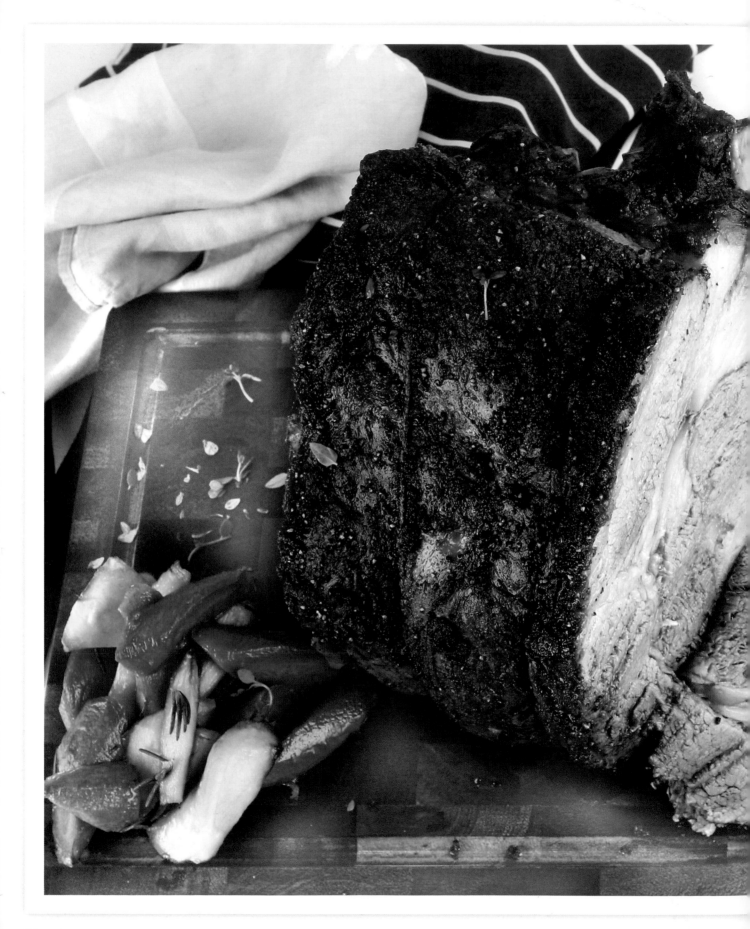

# THE PERFECT ROAST BEEF AND GRAVY

Sunday roast is one of my favourite meals to cook and nothing says Sunday roast better than a good joint of roast beef. I used a rib roast, which is my favourite.

**Prep time 25 mins ● Cook time 1hr 20mins ● Serves 6**

## INGREDIENTS

- 1.3kg-1.5kg of rib roast, on the bone
- 4 tbsp Derrycamma Farm Rapeseed Oil, plus a good drizzle
- 4 garlic cloves
- 3 medium onions
- 3 or 4 sprigs of fresh thyme
- 3 tsp cracked black pepper
- 2 tsp salt
- 2 tsp paprika
- 4 carrots (optional)
- 2 parsnips (optional)
- 50g butter
  Gravy
- 100ml red wine
- 50g flour
- 500ml boiling water
- ¼ tsp gravy browning

## METHOD

**1.** Allow the joint of beef to rest at room temperature for at least 45 minutes before starting.

**2.** Preheat the oven to 210°C or gas mark 7.

**3.** Peel the onion, carrots and parsnips, if using them, then cut into evenly-sized, large pieces.

**4.** Place the vegetables in the bottom of a roasting tin with the garlic and thyme then drizzle with a good drop of rapeseed oil. Set to one side.

**5.** Mix 3 tbsp of rapeseed oil with the pepper, salt and paprika, then rub this into the beef using your hands. Ensure it is coated really well - use more oil if you have to.

**6.** Heat a non-stick pan and seal the beef by placing it on the pan for about 45 seconds on each side. Remove from the pan and place on top of the vegetables in the roasting tin.

**7.** Place in the oven and turn the heat down to 180°C or gas mark 4, straight away.

**8.** Roast for 1 hour 10 minutes, ensuring you baste the beef with the cooking juices every 15 minutes. This will cook it rare. Cook for longer if you like it cooked more, I suggest 20+ minutes for medium and 35+ minutes for well done.

**9.** Add the butter for the last 15 minutes and baste again 5 minutes before removing from the oven, ensuring you coat the roast with as much butter and juices as possible.

**10.** Remove the beef from the roasting tin then leave on a plate to rest loosely covered with tin foil for 30 minutes before serving.

### Gravy

**1.** Place the roasting tin on a gas ring or electric hob and turn the heat to medium. Add the flour and, using a wooden spoon, ensure the flour absorbs as much of the melted butter and juices as possible. Cook out for about 1 minute then add the red wine and the 500ml of boiling water.

**2.** Bring to the boil and remove from the heat. Strain the contents of the roasting dish into a pot and put back on the heat.

**3.** Add the gravy browning and stir with a whisk then allow the gravy to reduce until it is at the consistency you like.

# SLOW COOKER BBQ BEEF SHORT RIBS

Beef ribs have more meat on them than their pork counterparts. Most people would be happy with 1 - carnivores like myself would go for 2-3. They make a great family dinner, aren't expensive and are easy to make in the slow cooker. They are also great when a few mates are coming round for some beers. Cook them in the slow cooker the day before then allow them to cool. Keep in the fridge overnight then stick them on the BBQ when your friends arrive. Give them about 15 minutes, turning often, all the while brushing them with lashings of the BBQ sauce. Your BBQs will become a very popular affair.

**Prep time 4-12 hours •**
**Cook time  2½-6 hours  •  Serves 2-5**

## INGREDIENTS

- **4 beef short ribs**
  **For the rub**
- **3 tbsp smoked paprika or paprika**
- **1 tsp cayenne pepper**
- **2 tsp ground cumin**
- **2 tbsp Muscovado sugar**
- **1 tbsp garlic powder**
- **1 tbsp salt**
  **For the BBQ sauce**
- **250g tomato ketchup**
- **100g Muscovado sugar**
- **2 tbsp white wine or cider vinegar**
- **2 tbsp Worcestershire or brown sauce**
- **1 x 500g carton tomato passata**
- **4 garlic cloves, finely chopped**
- **2 onions, finely chopped**

## METHOD

**1.** Mix all the rub ingredients together then rub it really well into each rib. Cover with cling film and leave in the fridge for at least 4 hours, ideally overnight.

**2.** Place them in your slow cooker, then mix the rest of the ingredients together in a bowl and pour on top of the ribs. You may need to add 100ml of water if the sauce doesn't cover the ribs at least half way.

**3.** Cover with the lid and turn the slow cooker to low and leave for 6 hours. If you are in a hurry, cook on high for 2½ hours. They are ready when the meat is almost ready to fall off the bone.

**4.** Remove the ribs from the cooker then either place on plates ready to serve immediately, roast in a pre-heated oven 180°C or gas mark 4 for 15–20 minutes or allow to cool for the BBQ.

**5.** To finish the sauce, transfer if from the slow cooker to a saucepan and bring to the boil. It should be nice and thick at this stage. If not, boil it for a few minutes until it thickens. Be careful of splashes as it will be extremely hot. Taste and adjust the seasoning. Pour on top of the melt-in-your-mouth ribs.

# BEEF LASAGNE

A good, homemade lasagne is such a warm, hearty dinner. Egg lasagne sheets are a little bit more expensive but taste better and I think they're worth it. This dish is brilliant for freezing, so you could also double the portions and freeze some for another day.

**Prep time 20 mins • Cook time 40 mins • Serves 6-8**

## INGREDIENTS

- 450g good quality steak mince
- 1 x 400g tin chopped tomatoes
- 500g tomato passata
- 10-15 lasagne sheets
- 4 garlic cloves, chopped
- 1 medium onion, finely chopped
- 1 tbsp dried oregano
- 1-2 large carrots, finely chopped
- 1 bell pepper, chopped
- 4 smoked rashers, chopped (optional)
- 1-2 good sized kale leaves, finely chopped
- 1 beef stock cube
- ¼ tsp black pepper
- 2 tbsp olive oil
- 100g cheddar cheese, grated
- 12 cherry
- tomatoes (optional)
  Cheese sauce
- 400ml milk
- 20g butter or margarine
- 20g plain flour
- 100g cheddar cheese, grated
- 1 vegetable stock cube

## METHOD

**1.** Heat the oil in the pan then fry the mince and rashers. Break it up so it is free from lumps.
**2.** When the mince is brown add the chopped vegetables and cook for 2-3 minutes.
**3.** Add the tin of chopped tomatoes, passata, oregano and stock cube. Stir well then turn the heat right down and simmer for 15 minutes.
**4.** Pre-heat your oven to 180°C or gas mark 4.
**5.** In the meantime, melt the butter in the microwave then add the flour and mix really well so they are combined to make a roux.
**6.** Heat the milk in the pot until it is almost boiling then add the cheese and the stock cube and stir well for about 1 minute.
**7.** Add half the roux and whisk until it is combined. This will will thicken the sauce. If it isn't thick enough, add more.
**8.** Remove both the meat sauce and cheese sauce from the heat and get a dish for your lasagne.
**9.** Spread a layer of the meat sauce on the bottom of the dish.
**10.** Add a layer of the lasagne sheets. Try not to overlap them as they may not cook through and don't be afraid to break a few sheets to make them fit.
**11.** Keep doing this until you have used all the mince and are left with a layer of lasagne sheets on top.
**12.** Pour the cheese sauce on top with the rest of the cheese. If using the cherry tomatoes, place them on top now.
**13.** Place onto a baking tray to catch any drips (and save you having to clean your oven) and bake for 20-25 minutes.
**14.** Remove from the oven and either serve immediately or allow to cool if you plan on freezing it.

*Liam's tip*
*Once cool it is really easy to cut and portion. Wrap each portion in cling film then freeze for up to 1 month. You can microwave it from frozen if the cling film is microwave safe.*

# Recipe notes

# Recipe notes

CHICKEN

# TANDOORI ROAST CHICKEN

Everyone loves a nice roast chicken. This is a twist on the one we are all used to. It makes a great family dinner and adds a bit of variety to your weekly menu. You can change the tandoori spice for Cajun or jerk seasoning. If you do, use natural yoghurt instead of Greek and also leave out the lemon juice.

**Prep time 10 mins • Marinating time 4-12 hours • Cook time 1½-2½ hours • Serves 4-6**

## INGREDIENTS
- 1 whole chicken, 1.4–1.9kg
- 50g plain flour
- 100g tandoori spice mix (found in Asian stores) or 100g tandoori curry powder (found in supermarkets)
- 50g Greek yoghurt
- 1 tsp salt
- Juice of ½ a lemon

## METHOD
**1.** Get all the ingredients ready before touching the raw chicken.
**2.** Mix the flour and salt with the tandoori spice then mix this with the lemon juice and yoghurt to form a paste. Leave it to one side.
**3.** Remove the chicken from the packaging and remove the elastic holding the legs in place.
**4.** Place the chicken in a large bowl then, using you hands, cover the entire bird in the paste you made. Cover the bowl with cling film then place in the fridge for at least 4 hours, preferably overnight.
**5.** Once the chicken has marinated, pre-heat your oven to 190°C or gas mark 5.
**6.** Place the chicken on a roasting tray then roast in the middle of the oven for 40 minutes per kilo, plus another 20 minutes. Make sure you baste the chicken by removing the roast from the oven then tipping it slightly. The juices will flow so use a soup spoon to scoop these over the chicken until you coat all of it. Return to the oven and repeat every 15 minutes.
**7.** Ensure the chicken is thoroughly cooked - the juices will run clear and there will be no pink meat.

# PILAU RICE

Even though I love plain boiled rice it can be a little boring so sometimes I make a lovely pilau rice as an alternative. It's pretty easy to make and only needs a few extra spices to give it a wonderfully fragrant flavour that goes really well with any curry or Indian dish.

**Prep time 5 mins • Cook time 10-15 mins • Serves 4**

## INGREDIENTS
- 450g basmati rice
- 1 small onion, finely chopped
- 2 garlic cloves, finely chopped
- 20g butter or ghee (a type of clarified butter)
- 2–3 bay leaves
- 550ml water
- 1 chicken or vegetable stock cube
- 6 whole cloves
- 1 small cinnamon stick
- 2 tsp turmeric
- 6 cardamom pods

## METHOD
**1.** Wash the rice thoroughly under a cold tap then leave to sit in water for 1 hour. This will remove the starch and give you fluffy rice.
**2.** Melt the butter in a heavy-bottomed pot, preferably one that has a lid.
**3.** Add the onion and garlic and slowly cook until softened and until they turn translucent in colour.
**4.** Drain the rice and add to the pot with the onion and garlic. Using a wooden spoon, stir it well so the butter coats the rice.
**4.** Place the cardamom pods on a chopping board and give then a whack with the flat side of a knife to release their flavour. Pop these, along with the cloves and turmeric, into the pot and stir well again.
**5.** Add the water and stock cube, stir until the cube dissolves then add the cinnamon stick.
**6.** Cover with a tight fitting lid or tin foil then simmer for 10 minutes until all the water has been absorbed.
**7.** Remove the cinnamon stick and give the rice a stir to fluff it up before serving.

# CHINESE FRIED CHICKEN WITH SWEET SOY AND CHILLI

**Prep time 15 mins • Cook time 20 mins • Serves 4**

## INGREDIENTS

- **4 chicken breasts**
- **200g flour**
- **50g cornflour**
- **2 tbsp Chinese five spice**
- **1 tsp ground ginger**
- **2 tbsp light soy sauce**
- **50ml sweet chilli sauce**
- **100g mange tout**
- **2 mixed peppers, diced**
- **1 onion, diced**
- **1 tbsp sesame or vegetable oil**

## METHOD

**1.** Pre-heat your oven to 180°C or gas mark 4 and turn your deep fat fryer to 180°C.

**2.** Cut the chicken breasts into cubes. You should get 6-8 from each.

**3.** Place them in a bowl of cold water ensuring they are totally submerged.

**4.** Mix the flour, cornflour, ground ginger and Chinese five spice in another bowl.

**5.** Remove a few pieces of chicken from the water and roll them in the flour mix so they are completely coated. Place them on a plate and repeat until all the chicken has been coated.

**6.** Place the chicken into the deep fat fryer, ensuring you don't overload the basket. Cook for about 2 minutes, until the chicken is crispy.

**7.** Heat 1 tbsp of the oil in a pan then add all the vegetables and mange tout. Sauté for around 4 minutes then add the chicken and cook for another 2 minutes before adding the soy sauce and sweet chilli sauce.

**8.** Transfer everything into an ovenproof dish and bake, uncovered, for 10-15 minutes. Check the chicken is cooked by cutting into a large piece and making sure there's no pink.

**9.** Stir well to ensure the chicken and vegetables are totally coated in the sauce.

■ *Serve with rice, noodles or a nice salad.*

# Southern Fried Chicken

**Prep time 15 mins** ●
**Cook time 25-35mins** ●
**Serves 2-4**

## INGREDIENTS
- 10 chicken drumsticks, thighs
  or a mix of each
- 200g plain flour
- 50g cornflour
- 3 tbsp cracked black pepper
- 1 tsp garlic powder
- ½ tsp salt
- 500ml cold water

## METHOD
**1.** Pre-heat your oven to 180°C or gas mark 4 and turn your deep fat fryer to 170°C.

**2.** Place the water in a bowl, then add the chicken pieces.

**3.** In a separate bowl, mix the rest of the dry ingredients together. Get a plate ready and leave it beside the dry mix.

**4.** One by one, take a piece of chicken from the water then roll it in the dry mix until it is completely coated. Place on the plate then repeat until you coat all the chicken pieces.

**5.** Place 2 or 3 pieces into the fryer, ensuring the basket isn't overloaded. The oil needs to be able to move around the chicken. Cook until it's crisp - this usually takes 2-3 minutes.

**6.** Place a sheet of greaseproof paper on a baking tray then place the chicken from the fryer on this.

**7.** When all the chicken is coated and nice and crispy place the baking tray in the oven for 20-25 minutes.

**8.** It is so important the chicken is cooked through so check a piece to make sure. The juices should run clear with no trace of blood or pink in them.

## Thai Fried Chicken
- 200g flour
- 50g cornflour
- 2 tsp ground ginger
- 1 tsp ground coriander
- Zest of 1 lime
- ½ tsp chilli powder
  (use more if you like it hotter)
- Bunch of fresh coriander, chopped

## METHOD
**1.** Follow the same steps as Southern Fried Chicken.

## Tandoori Fried Chicken
- 200g flour
- 50g cornflour
- 6 tbsp tandoori seasoning (found in Asian stores) or 6 tbsp tandoori curry powder (found in supermarkets)

## METHOD
**1.** Follow the same steps as Southern Fried Chicken.

# CAJUN CHICKEN BURGERS

Chicken burgers always seem to come with some sort of crumb. This is done to add bulk so they can use less chicken. This recipe uses a whole chicken breast so you know exactly what you are eating. Processed burgers don't even come close to how delicious this is.

## INGREDIENTS

- **4 chicken breasts**
- **4 tbsp Cajun seasoning + 2 tsp for the sauce**
- **4 burger baps**
- **5 tbsp crème fraiche**
- **2 large tomatoes, sliced**
- **1 pepper, sliced**
- **1 onion, thinly sliced**
- **5 tbsp olive oil**
- **Handful of rocket or mixed leaves**

## METHOD

**1.** Pre-heat your oven to 180°C or gas mark 4.

**2.** Butterfly the chicken breasts. Do this by laying the chicken breast flat and start cutting sideways through the thinner side of the breast. Don't cut all the way through. Open the breast up so the fold is facing up (like opening a book) and the original top of the breast is laying face down on the chopping board.

**3.** Mix 3 tbsp of olive oil and 4 tbsp of Cajun seasoning in a bowl. Roll each breast in this mix so cach is totally coated in the Cajun spice.

**4.** Heat 2 tbsp olive oil in a pan. Without overloading the pan, seal each breast for about 1 minute on each side.

**5.** Place the chicken on a baking tray then bake for 15–20 minutes, depending on the size of the breasts. Ensure they are fully cooked by cutting into the thickest part. Make sure there is no pink meat whatsoever and that the juices are clear.

**6.** In a cup or bowl mix the crème fraiche with the remaining 2 tsp of Cajun seasoning.

**7.** Toast the burger baps then place the bottom bun on a plate. Coat each in a little sauce then add slices of tomato and onion followed by some lettuce leaves and the sliced peppers. Place the burger on top of this followed by a good dollop of sauce then the top of the bap.

■ ***Perfect with sweet potato fries and a nice salad.***

# CHICKEN CASSOULET

This classic French dish gets its name from the dish it is cooked in. Traditionally it was cooked in a heavy cast iron pot with a lid, often over an open fire. It's basically the French version of one of our stews. This version is cheaper because it uses chicken thighs and legs with regular breakfast sausages instead of the pricier smoked sausage. The smoked paprika will give the dish that extra flavour.

**Prep time 15 mins ●
Cook time 1½ hours ● Serves 4-6**

## INGREDIENTS

- 8-12 chicken drumsticks and thighs
- 1lb sausages (breakfast style)
- 4 garlic cloves, chopped
- 2 medium onions, sliced
- 1 large beetroot, peeled and cut in chunks
- 2 large carrots
- 4 sprigs of thyme, stalks removed
- 8–10 sundried tomatoes
- 1 tbsp Dijon mustard
- 500g tomato passata
- 300ml water
- 1 tbsp smoked paprika
- ½ tsp freshly ground black pepper
- 1 chicken stock cube
- 200g button mushrooms (optional)

## METHOD

**1.** Pre-heat your oven to 180°C or gas mark 4.

**2.** Peel the carrots and cut into random chunks around the same size as half a sausage.

**3.** Heat the oil in a pan and fry the sausages until evenly brown all over.

**4.** Using the same pan, brown the chicken. It doesn't have to be fully cooked at this point.

**5.** Place the chicken in an earthenware pot, casserole dish or a slow cooker with the sausages and the rest of the ingredients and stir well.

**6.** Cover and place in the oven for 1 hour 30 minutes. If using your slow cooker, cook on low for 5 hours or high for 1 hour 30 minutes.

**7.** Taste, adjust seasoning if needed and serve.

■ *This tastes great with crusty bread or baby new potatoes with a dollop of butter melting over them*.

*Vegetarian alternative*
Use lentils and butter beans instead of the chicken and sausage.

## Vegetarian alternative

To make a vegetarian version, use the same ingredients but substitute the chicken for 300g of tofu or 150g of aubergine and 150g of courgette. If using the tofu, cut it into medium-sized cubes. If using vegetables, cut them into extra large chunks. Follow the exact same method as above, but reduce the oven time to 10 minutes.

# HEALTHY CHICKEN AND PASTA BAKE

This is a healthy midweek meal that your family will love. It's bursting with fresh flavours and its vibrant colours also make it a feast for the eyes. It can easily be adapted to suit your own taste - you can change the vegetables to include your favourites.

**Prep time 15 mins • Cook time 20 mins • Serves 4-6**

## INGREDIENTS

- **4 chicken breasts**
- **2 garlic cloves**
- **¼ red chilli, seeds removed (optional but recommended)**
- **15–20 basil leaves**
- **2 peppers (mix the colours for**
- **presentation)**
- **1 red onion**
- **10–15 cherry tomatoes**
- **400g penne pasta**
- **¼ tsp freshly ground black pepper**
- **Pinch of salt**
- **20g fresh parmesan cheese, grated**
- **30ml olive oil**

## METHOD

**1.** Cook the pasta as per the packet instructions. When cooked, cool under a cold running tap and drain then pour about 1 tbsp olive oil over the top and mix in. Washing it removes the starch and the oil stops it sticking together.

**2.** Pre-heat your oven to 180°C or gas mark 4.

**3.** Place the garlic, 1 small slice of green pepper, half the basil, the ground pepper and chilli into a blender with the remaining olive oil and blitz until smooth.

**4.** Cut the chicken into cubes - you should get about 8 from each. Place in a bowl and coat the chicken in the mixture from step 3. Mix well and set to one side. Clean your board, knife and hands really well after cutting the chicken.

**5.** Cut the peppers and onion into cubes around the same size as the chicken.

**6.** Heat the pan and add the chicken and oil mix. Cook for 2 minutes until the chicken starts to colour, then add the vegetables and cook for a further 5 minutes.

**7.** Remove from the heat then mix in the pasta and cherry tomatoes

**8.** Place in a casserole dish and bake for 15 minutes. Check the chicken is cooked, and if so, remove from the oven, mix in the grated parmesan and the rest of the basil leaves and serve.

# KUNG PO CHICKEN

This simple Chinese dish is extremely popular. It is made a little differently here in Ireland than I have seen it made abroad - for example in Hong Kong and other places they use peanuts.

**Prep time 15 mins • Cook time 25 mins • Serves 4**

## INGREDIENTS
- 4 chicken breasts
- 2 peppers
- 1 onion
- 4 spring onions
- 2 tbsp oil
- 50g beans sprouts (optional)
- 50g unsalted peanuts (though salted will do)
  The sauce
- 2 tbsp sugar
- 1 tbsp dark soy sauce
- 1 tbsp white vinegar
- 2 tbsp tomato ketchup
- 2 garlic cloves, finely chopped
- ½ inch fresh ginger, finely chopped
- ½ red chilli, seeds removed unless you like it hot
- 2 tbsp cornflour

## METHOD
1. Add all the sauce ingredients, except the cornflour, to a pot and bring to the boil. Reduce heat, then simmer for 10 minutes.
2. Mix the cornflour with 1 tsp of water to form a paste. Whisk the paste into the sauce and bring back to the boil. Remove from the heat and leave to one side.
3. Cut the chicken into a medium dice. You should get around 8 pieces from a breast. Cut the vegetables into a similar size.
4. Heat the oil in a pan, then add the chicken. Cook for 5 minutes, then add the vegetables and cook for a further 5 minutes.
5. Add the sauce and simmer for 5 minutes. Add the peanuts and beansprouts and give it one final stir.

■ *Serve with boiled rice or chips.*

# SWEET AND SOUR CHICKEN IN CRISPY BATTER

Sweet and sour sauce is a firm favourite in lots of families. This is the crispy chicken version that a lot of takeaways serve - and of course this one is much tastier and healthier.

**Prep time 15 mins** ● **Cook time 25 mins** ● **Serves 4**

## INGREDIENTS
- **4 chicken breasts**
- **30g cornflour**
  **The batter**
- **225g plain flour**
- **50g cornflour**
- **300ml ice cold soda water or sparkling water (tap water will do)**
  **The sauce**
- **250ml pineapple juice or water**
- **2 tbsp sugar (8 if using water)**
- **2 tbsp white vinegar**
- **4 tbsp tomato ketchup**
- **2 tbsp cornflour**

## METHOD
### The batter
**1.** Turn your deep fat fryer on to 170°C.

**2.** Mix all the batter ingredients together in a bowl. I use a hand blender to speed it up.

### The sauce
**1.** Add all the sauce ingredients, except the cornflour, to a pot and bring to the boil. Reduce heat, then simmer for 10 minutes.

**2.** Mix the cornflour with 2 tsp of water to form a paste. Whisk the paste into the sauce and bring back to the boil. Remove from the heat and leave to one side.

### Putting it together
**1.** Pre-heat your oven to 180°C or gas mark 4.

**2.** Slice the chicken breasts in half lengthwise, then turn to the side and cut them into cubes. You should end up with around 8.

**3.** Roll the chicken in the cornflour.

**4.** One by one, dip each piece into the batter mix, then slowly drop into the fryer. Don't overload the fryer or they will stick together. You will have to cook them in batches. They may stick to the basket so the best way to avoid this is to ensure the basket is lowered before adding the chicken.

**5.** Cook for about 2-3 minutes. Then place on a baking tray lined with greaseproof paper.

**6.** Pop them into the oven for 10–15 minutes when done.

■ **Serve with boiled rice and the sauce on the side.**

### Liam's tip
*If the chicken sticks to the basket, scrape the batter from under the basket and the chicken will come free*

# THAI GREEN CURRY

This is probably the most popular of all Thai curries. I always prefer to make my own paste but it's not always possible due to the availability of ingredients. So shop-bought paste is totally fine and will be delicious too. I usually end up adding extra spices and flavours to it whenever making this dish.

**Prep time 20-25 min • Marinating 4 hours • Cook time 25-35 mins • Serves 4**

## INGREDIENTS

**If making your own paste use:**
- **8 fresh green chillies (remove the seeds unless you want it very hot)**
- **1 tsp ground coriander**
- **Small handful of fresh coriander**
- **1 tsp ground cumin**
- **2 tsp white peppercorns**
- **½ tsp salt**
- **8 garlic cloves**
- **1 inch of ginger or galangal**
- **3 inches lemongrass, chopped**
- **2 tsp shrimp paste**
- **Zest of half a lime plus 2 tsp of juice**
- **2 shallots or 1 small onion**
  **Or use shop bought paste and use the recommended amount**

  **The Rest**
- **2 x 400g tins coconut milk**
- **4 chicken breasts**
- **1 medium onion, sliced**
- **1–2 peppers, sliced**
- **10–15 fresh basil leaves**
- **1 chicken stock cube (optional)**
- **1–2 tbsp coconut oil or peanut oil (sunflower or vegetable oil will do)**

## METHOD
### The paste
**1.** Place the white peppercorns, cumin, ground coriander, green chillies and salt into a pestle and mortar and grind for about 5 minutes.
**2.** Add the garlic, galangal or ginger, lime zest, fresh coriander, shallots and lemongrass then grind for about 10 minutes, or until they have started to form a paste.
**3.** Add the lime juice and shrimp paste then gently pound for about 5 minutes more, until you have a thick paste.
**4.** Alternatively, add all the paste ingredients to the food processor and blitz until smooth.

### The curry
**1.** Cut the chicken into cubes.
**2.** Slice the peppers and onion on a different chopping board with a different knife to prevent cross contamination.
**3.** Place the chicken in a bowl and add 2 tbsp of the paste, mix really well then cover and leave in the fridge for at least 4 hours (you can use it immediately but it won't be as nice)
**4.** Heat 1 tbsp of oil in a wok or a pan then add the chicken and cook right through, stirring continuously. Remove and set to one side.
**5.** Heat a little oil in the wok then add 2-5 tbsp of the lovely paste you made or from the jar you bought.
**6.** Stir the paste continuously. Add the peppers and onion after about 1 minute. Keep stirring and cook for 2 minutes more.
**7.** Add the coconut milk and basil leaves and simmer for 15 minutes. You can add a chicken stock cube if you like.
**8.** Place the chicken into the sauce and heat for another 10 minutes. Taste and adjust the seasoning.
■ *Serve with jasmine or basmati rice.*

# THE PERFECT ROAST CHICKEN

Roast chicken is one of those dishes that almost everyone loves. It's great for a Sunday roast and just as good as a midweek meal. It is also ideal for sandwiches or for adding to a curry.

**Prep time 10 mins ● Cook time 1 hour 45 mins ● Serves 4-6**

## INGREDIENTS

- 1.4kg or 1 medium chicken
- 6 smoked back bacon rashers or 10-12 smoked streaky rashers
- 5 tbsp Derrycamma Farm Rape-seed Oil
- 2 garlic cloves, finely chopped
- 25g butter
- Pinch of salt and pepper
- Sage and Onion Stuffing from page 196

## METHOD

**1.** Pre-heat your oven to 180°C or gas mark 4.
**2.** Soften the butter slightly, then add the salt, pepper and garlic. Mix really well then set to one side.
**3.** Remove the chicken from any packaging. Don't wash it as you could easily spread harmful bacteria all over your kitchen. Simply remove the string from the legs and check that the cavity is empty.
**4.** Stuff the chicken through its neck cavity with the Sage and Onion Stuffing, packing it right in.
**5.** Just above where you stuffed the chicken, you will see the top of the breast. Gently use your fingers to part the skin from the flesh. Start right in the middle and work your way back. Don't remove it, just separate it.
**6.** Take the butter and rub it underneath the skin and when done, pat the skin back into its original position.
**7.** Run the oil all over the bird, then wash your hands really well with antibacterial soap. Make sure you don't touch anything else until your hands are washed and dried.
**8.** Layer the rashers over the chicken, starting at the back and working your way forward to where you stuffed it and put the butter. You don't have to cover the legs. Keep one rasher back to cover the cavity where you put the stuffing.
**9.** Cover the roasting tin and bird with foil and place in the oven for 30 minutes.
**10.** Remove from the oven and gently remove the foil, try not to tear it as you want to cover the bird again. Using a soup spoon or baster, scoop up some of the cooking juices and baste the chicken. This helps keep the meat nice and moist.
**11.** Cover again and cook for a further 30 minutes. Repeat this once more, so it has been in the oven for one and a half hours and basted twice.
**12.** Remove the foil and baste again. Turn the oven up to 200°C or gas mark 6 and roast the chicken uncovered for 15 minutes.
**13.** Remove the chicken from the oven and allow the meat to rest for 10-15 minutes before serving.

### Liam's tip

*I always use a meat thermometer to test the meat temperature has reached 75°C. If you don't have one then pierce the flesh at the thickest part with a skewer or knife and ensure the juices are golden and clear of blood or any pink. Test just below the leg the same way.*

# Recipe notes

# Recipe notes

PORK

# RUSTIC ITALIAN SMOKED HAM STEW
## (Gluten free)

Prep time 20 mins •
Cook time 2 hours • Serves 4-6

## INGREDIENTS

- 400g piece of smoked ham
- 1 tsp English mustard
- ½ red onion
- ½ white onion
- 1 courgette
- ½ aubergine
- 1 red pepper
- 1 vegetable, chicken or ham stock cube
- ¼ savoy cabbage
- 1x400g tin white butter beans
- 500g tomato passata
- Handful of fresh basil leaves
- Parmesan cheese to top
- Freshly ground black pepper
- For lactose free, leave out the cheese.
- For coeliacs, please ensure your mustard and stock cubes are gluten free.

## METHOD

1. Pre-heat the oven to 180°C or gas mark 4.
2. Place the ham in a medium pot, cover with water then bring to the boil and simmer for 1.5 hours. Remove to a plate and allow to cool.
3. When the ham has cooled, shred into 1-2 inch pieces, then place in a casserole dish.
4. Cut the vegetables into 1 inch pieces and add these to the same casserole dish.
5. Pour the tomato passata over the top then crumble the stock cube into the dish and add the black pepper. Place in the oven for 20 minutes.

■ *Serve with crusty bread or penne or fusilli pasta.*

*Liam's tip*
*You can add peeled baby new potatoes or salad potatoes when you're adding the vegetables for a heartier dish. Or for a delicious vegetarian stew, simply leave out the ham.*

# PORK FILLET MEDALLIONS, CREAMY MASH AND MUSHROOM SAUCE

## (Gluten free)

I often see pork fillets on offer in butchers and supermarkets. They don't look very big but believe me, you will feed a family fairly easily with one. If you don't know how to trim a whole fillet and cut it into medallions then ask your butcher to do it for you.

**Prep time 15 mins •**
**Cook time 15 mins • Serves 4-6**

## INGREDIENTS

- **1 pork fillet or 3–4 medallions per person**
- **2 tbsp paprika**
- **½ tsp freshly ground black pepper**
- **½ tsp salt**
- **Perfect Mash from p184**
  **The sauce**
- **250ml cream**
- **200g button mushrooms, sliced**
- **1 shallot or small onion, finely chopped**
- **1 garlic clove, finely chopped**
- **1 tsp Dijon mustard**
- **¼ vegetable stock cube**
- **4 tbsp olive oil**
- **Fresh parsley, chopped**

## METHOD

**1.** Fold a piece of cling film over itself at least 3 times so that you end up with a piece about half an A4 page in size.
**2.** Place a medallion flat side down on one side of the cling film.
**3.** Fold it over the medallion then beat with a meat hammer or rolling pin. You want it to almost double in size. Do this for each medallion.
**4.** Mix the paprika, pepper and salt in a bowl then add 3 tbsp of olive oil. Coat each medallion with this mix.
**5.** Add 1 tbsp of oil to a pot then add the garlic, onion or shallot, and sliced mushrooms. Cook for 2 minutes without colouring.
**6.** Add the cream, mustard and ¼ stock cube.
**7.** Boil until the cream thickens, then remove from the heat. Taste and adjust seasoning if necessary.
**8.** Heat a pan then cook each pork medallion for about 2 minutes each side.
**9.** Place a dollop of mash on the center of the plate then top this with 3 or 4 medallions of pork. Drizzle the sauce around the plate and sprinkle with some chopped parsley.

## Liam's tip
*You can make a vegetarian alternative to this recipe by using thick slices of Portobello mushrooms, aubergine and courgettes instead of the pork medallions. Roll in the oil and seasoning then grill or pan-fry.*

# PORK AND APPLE BURGERS

**Prep time 15 mins • Cook time 15 mins • Serves 6**

## INGREDIENTS

- 450g minced pork
- 100g smoked rashers
- 1 cooking or Granny Smith apple
- 2 tsp wholegrain mustard
- 3 tsp paprika
- 1 tsp freshly ground black pepper
- 6 brioche buns
- Lettuce and tomato for topping
- 6 tbsp mayonnaise
- 3 tbsp tomato ketchup
- 2 tbsp oil

## METHOD

**1.** Pre-heat your oven to 180°C or gas mark 4.

**2.** Chop the rashers into thin strips. Peel, core and chop the apple into small pieces.

**3.** Place the pork in a bowl and add the rashers, apple, paprika, pepper and mustard. Mix really well.

**4.** Get a plate ready beside the bowl then, using your hands, divide the mixture into 6 portions. Shape each into a burger.

**5.** Heat 2 tbsp of oil on a pan then flash fry the burgers for about 1 minute on each side. They should be nicely browned. Place them on a baking tray and pop into the oven for 15 minutes.

**6.** Mix the mayonnaise and ketchup together in a cup and lightly toast the brioche buns.

**7.** When the buns are toasted, add a dollop of the sauce. Top this with a burger, some crispy lettuce and juicy tomatoes, followed another good dollop of the sauce before adding the top of the bun.

■ *Serve with chunky chips, sweet potato fries or a nice salad.*

# VEGETARIAN PORTOBELLO MUSHROOM BURGER

I couldn't do a pile of burgers and not include a vegetarian recipe - I'd never hear the end of it from some of my BiaMaith friends and followers. So to keep from getting in trouble, here is a veggie burger that I'm sure everyone will really enjoy. This is tasty with a simple green salad as it allows the flavours in the burger to shine. Dress it with some of the oil you marinate the mushroom in, and fresh basil leaves with a hint of balsamic vinegar.

**Prep time 15 min • Marinating time 4-12 hours •
Cook Time 15 mins • Serves 4**

## INGREDIENTS
- 4 large portobello mushrooms
- 200ml olive oil
- 4 garlic cloves, finely chopped
- ½ tsp fresh nutmeg, finely grated
- 10 fresh basil leaves, finely chopped
- ¼ tsp freshly ground black pepper
- 2 tsp tomato purée or paste
- 1 tsp chilli powder (optional)
- 4 burger buns or baps
- 2 large tomatoes, thinly sliced
- 1 red onion, thinly sliced
- 1 roasted red pepper (optional)
- 15 hazelnuts (optional)
- 6 tbsp crème fraiche
- Handful of rocket leaves

## METHOD
**1.** Mix half of the chopped garlic with 50ml of olive oil then add the nutmeg, basil and tomato purée. Set aside.
**2.** Pour the rest of the oil into a bowl large enough to hold the mushrooms. Mix in the rest of the garlic and the chilli powder, if using it.
**3.** Roll each mushroom in this oil really well then cover with cling film and leave to marinate for 4 hours at room temperature or 12 hours in the fridge.
**4.** Pre-heat your oven to 180°C or gas mark 4.
**5.** Remove the mushrooms from the oil and allow to drain well. I dab them on some kitchen paper.
**6.** Using a pastry brush or your clean fingers, brush the mix you made in step 1 over each mushroom, then place on a baking tray and bake for 10-15 minutes.
**7.** If using the hazelnuts, blend them in a food processor until almost dust. Mix this with the crème fraiche. If not then mix a hint ¼ tsp of nutmeg in instead. If you're serving this to guests, warn them that it contains nuts just in case of an allergy.
**8.** Toast the burger buns. Coat the bottom bun in the crème fraiche sauce, ensuring you keep a good bit aside to coat the top. Add the tomatoes then the rocket, followed by the red onion and the roasted pepper, if using.
**9.** Place the mushroom on top of this, then more sauce and finally the top of the bun.

# BOILED BACON AND CABBAGE

How could I write a family cookbook and not include this traditional favourite? I nearly always go for this option if I see it on a carvery menu when I'm eating out. Not everywhere serves it with parsley sauce though - and gravy with bacon and cabbage is just wrong in my book. Cabbage itself isn't a great tasting vegetable unless it's cooked properly. Cook it in the bacon water or a vegetable stock cube and you'll see a huge difference in the flavour.

**Prep time 4 hours 15 mins •**
**Cook time 1 hour 20 mins • Serves 4-6**

## INGREDIENTS
- **1kg back bacon joint**
- **300ml milk**
- **1 York or Savoy cabbage**
- **25g flour**
- **45g butter or margarine**
- **1 vegetable stock cube**
- **Pinch of freshly ground black pepper**
- **Small bunch of fresh parsley, chopped**

## METHOD
**1.** Cover the bacon with cold water and soak for about 4 hours. This removes the salt left over from curing the bacon.
**2.** Pop the bacon on to boil, then turn the heat down and simmer for 1 hour and 20 minutes.
**3.** Drain the water off into another pot then re-cover the bacon with fresh water.
**4.** Cut the cabbage into quarters then cut the hard stalk piece from each. Turn sideways and shred into thin strips, wash well then place into the water you drained off the bacon earlier. Cook for 10-15 minutes.

**5.** Place the milk in a saucepan and slowly bring to the boil.
**6.** Melt just over half the butter in another pot then add the flour and cook out for about 1 minute stirring all the time to make a roux.
**7.** Add the stock cube to the milk then whisk in the roux until free from lumps. Taste, and add more salt and pepper if needed, or a little milk if it's too thick. Add the chopped parsley and stir. You can pass it through a sieve or use a stick blender if you end up with a lumpy sauce.
**8.** When the bacon is cooked remove from the water and allow to rest on a plate for 10 minutes.
**9.** Drain the cabbage from the water and place back in the pot, add the rest of the butter and a pinch of salt and pepper before stirring well. .
**10.** Place a spoon of cabbage beside this then spoon a little sauce over the top and serve.
■ *Serve with a a dollop of mash and drizzle with a generous portion of your parsley sauce.*

# BACON AND CABBAGE PIE

Every now and then I find I have leftovers after making bacon and cabbage. It doesn't happen often as I usually eat too much when I make it - I seriously love a proper bacon and cabbage. Sometimes, though, I cook it just to make this pie. It's a really unusual one, but trust me, it's fantastic. It's delicious on its own, or you can eat it cold with a salad.

**Prep time 1 hour 20 mins •**
**Cook time 25-30 mins • Serves 4 -6**

## INGREDIENTS
Bacon and Cabbage from page 119
For the pastry
- 250g plain flour
- 125g butter or margarine
- 1 egg + 1 for the egg wash
- 2 tsp cold water
- Pinch of salt

## METHOD
**1.** Cook the bacon and cabbage. Don't forget to make the parsley sauce as well. Allow all the ingredients to cool.
**2.** Add the flour and salt to a bowl, then, using the tips of your fingers, rub the butter into the flour until you are left with a fine sand-like crumb.
**3.** Add the egg and mix in using a cold, metal spoon or the flat side of a knife. If it needs more liquid, add the water. When it forms a dough, wrap it in cling film then place in the fridge for 1–2 hours.
**4.** When ready, remove the pastry from the fridge and pre-heat your oven to 180°C or gas mark 4.
**5.** Cut the dough in two even pieces. Roll one out a little larger than your pie dish. Gently and loosely fold the pastry and place it over the dish, then unfold it so it covers the whole dish. Press the dough into the edges lightly.
**6.** Break the bacon apart with your hands or cut it into cubes with a knife.
**7.** Add a layer of bacon to the bottom of the dish, then a layer of cabbage then a layer of sauce. Repeat until the dish is full to the top.
**8.** Roll out the other piece of pastry so it is a little larger than the top of the dish.
**9.** Beat the second egg in a cup then, using a pastry brush,

brush the sides of the pastry lining the dish.
**10.** Place the top layer of pastry on by picking it up with your rolling pin. Press down on the sides to bind the pastry, then press down lightly with a fork all the way around. Cut away any excess pastry.
**11.** Using your pastry brush, brush the top of the pie with egg. Pop into the oven on a middle shelf for 15 minutes.
**12.** Remove from the oven and brush with egg once more. Then stick it back in the oven for a further 10–15 minutes.

■ *Serve with a nice ploughman's lunch or a salad. I love it with a big plate of creamy mash.*

# CHAR SUI PORK BELLY

I learned this recipe from a friend in mainland China and it's my favourite roast pork dish. It's an old family recipe passed down through generations. I love the flavours and it tastes nothing like the dried out Char Sui most Chinese take aways serve. It's succulent on the inside with a really rich, crispy, burnt caramel flavour on the outside.

**Prep time 15 mins • Marinating time 4 hours • Cook time 45-60 mins • Serves 6-8**

## INGREDIENTS
- 1 kg–2 kg pork belly, rind removed
- ½ inch of fresh ginger, chopped
- 2 garlic cloves, finely chopped
- 2 tbsp Chinese rice wine or sherry
- 3 tbsp hoi sin sauce
- 2 tbsp sesame oil
- 3 tbsp muscovado sugar

## METHOD
**1.** Mix all the ingredients together in a small bowl then place the pork in a large bowl or roasting tin.
**2.** Rub the mixture into the pork belly, ensuring you coat every inch of it.
**3.** Leave in the bowl or tin, cover with cling film and return to the fridge for 4 hours or better yet, overnight.
**4.** Pre-heat your oven to 160°C or gas mark 3.
**5.** Place the pork fat side up in a roasting tin. Roast in the oven for 45–60 minutes (depending on size) or until the top starts to turn really dark and crispy.
**6.** Remove from the oven and remove the pork from the tin: Place on a cutting board or plate and let the pork rest for 15 minutes while covered loosely with foil.
**7.** Slice the meat as thinly as you possibly can otherwise the burnt sugar taste will overpower the flavour of the meat.

### Liam's tip
*You can serve this with stir-fried vegetables or with an Asian salad of grated carrot, shredded white cabbage, bean sprouts and onion. Make a dressing with 1 tsp of soy sauce, 1 tsp of sesame oil, 1 tsp of Chinese rice wine or sherry, a pinch of freshly chopped ginger, coriander, ¼ of chilli finely chopped and ½ a clove of crushed garlic.*

# BACON AND MUSHROOM PASTA

Sometimes it can be hard to please everyone in the family at dinner time. This is one of those dishes that can easily be adapted to suit everyone. Leave the bacon out for vegetarians, use crème fraiche for a lower fat version, or use gluten free pasta if needed. You can add roasted peppers, spinach or even frozen peas to up the vegetable intake.

**Prep time 10 mins •**
**Cook time 15 mins • Serves 2-3**

## INGREDIENTS
- 200g penne pasta or similar
- 200g button mushrooms, chopped
- 250ml fresh cream
- 200g smoked rashers, bacon lardons or pancetta, sliced into thin strips
- 1 garlic clove, chopped
- ½ tsp dried oregano
- 2 tbsp and 1 tsp olive oil
- ½ onion, sliced
- 50g fresh parmesan, ½ for the sauce and ½ to serve

## METHOD
**1.** Cook the pasta as per the instructions on the packet. Drain the water and rinse under a cold tap until cooled. This removes the starch. Add 1 tsp of olive oil and leave to one side.
**2.** Heat the remaining olive oil on a pan and add the bacon. Cook for 1-2 minutes, then add the garlic, onion and mushrooms. Cook for about 3 minutes until the onions are soft and the mushrooms have cooked.
**3.** Add the black pepper and the cream, stir and allow to reduce and thicken.
**4.** Add the pasta to the sauce then stir well until the sauce coats the pasta and it's nice and hot.
**5.** Sprinkle with a touch of grated parmesan, stir, adjust seasoning and dish up. I always add a sprinkle of parmesan cheese to the top before serving.

# SPAGHETTI AMATRICIANA

This is another simple and inexpensive pasta dish based on my Napoletana sauce. It makes a great family dish that takes very little effort. It's cheaper and a lot tastier than the jars available in supermarkets. And best of all, it's much better for you, too.

Prep time 10 minutes •
Cook time 10 minutes • Serves 4–6

## INGREDIENTS

- 400g spaghetti or linguine
- 200g smoked pancetta or smoked bacon lardons (smoked rashers will do)
- ½ red chilli, finely chopped (de-seeded if you don't want it hot)
- Napoletana Sauce (page 210)
- 50g Pecorino, grated or 50g fresh parmesan, grated cheese, grated
- 3 tbsp olive oil

## METHOD

1. Cook the pasta as per the instructions on the packet. Cool down under running cold water and drain. Mix in 1 tbsp of olive oil and set to one side.
2. Half fill the pot you cooked the pasta in with hot water and place on the boil.
3. Heat the reamining oil in a pan then add the diced pancetta, lardons or rashers.
4. Cook until almost crispy, then add the chopped chilli. Cook for 1-2 minutes more, then add a little bit of water to de-glaze the pan. De-glazing a pan means adding liquid while the pan is hot which lifts the flavour that has transferred to the surface of the pan.
5. Add the Napoletana Sauce to the pan, then allow to simmer for 10 minutes.
6. Meanwhile, put the cooked pasta back into the pot of water for 1 minute, then drain and add to the sauce.
7. Mix really well, then top with grated cheese. Mix some more, taste to adjust the seasoning and serve.

# BANGERS AND MASH WITH ONION GRAVY

You can buy expensive sausages to make this dish and they will be lovely. I make it with regular sausages you can find in almost every shop in Ireland. My mum used to make this and she served it with white pudding and rashers. I loved it. I savoured every bite as if I were eating a fillet steak. It's one of those dinners that I cook for the homely comfort feeling it gives me as much as for the lovely flavours.

**Prep time 15 mins ●**
**Cook time 10-15 mins ● Serves 4**

## INGREDIENTS
- **1-2lb sausages**
- **8 rashers (optional)**
- **8 pieces of white pudding  (optional)**
- **Mash from page 184**
- **2 tbsp olive oil Homemade Gravy**
- **1 beef stock pot or stock cube**
- **300ml water**
- **1 tbsp tomato puree or paste**
- **2 tsp gravy browning**
- **6 tbsp Onion Marmalade from page 219 (optional) or 1 medium onion, sliced and fried for 2 minutes**
- **20g flour**
- **20g butter or margarine**
- **Gravy granules (optional, if using, leave out the flour and butter)**

## METHOD
**1.** If using gravy granules, follow the instructions on the packet then add the Onion Marmalade or the fried onions, and simmer.
**2.** Make the mash.
**3.** Skip this step if you used gravy granules otherwise, melt the butter in a pot then add the flour, keep on a medium heat for 1 minute stirring all the time. Add the rest of the gravy ingredients and whisk or blitz with a stick blender until all the lumps have gone. Add the onion marmalade or fried onions then bring to the boil and turn down to a simmer.
**4.** Heat the oil in a pan and fry the sausages. Turn them regularly and keep the heat at medium so they don't burn. They should cook in about 10 minutes.
**5.** Cook the rashers and pudding now if you're using them.
**6.** Taste the gravy, adjust seasoning if necessary.
**7.** Place a dollop of mash on the plate then pop the sausages on top of this followed by a drizzle of gravy around the plate.

# Recipe notes

# Recipe notes

# Recipe notes

TURKEY

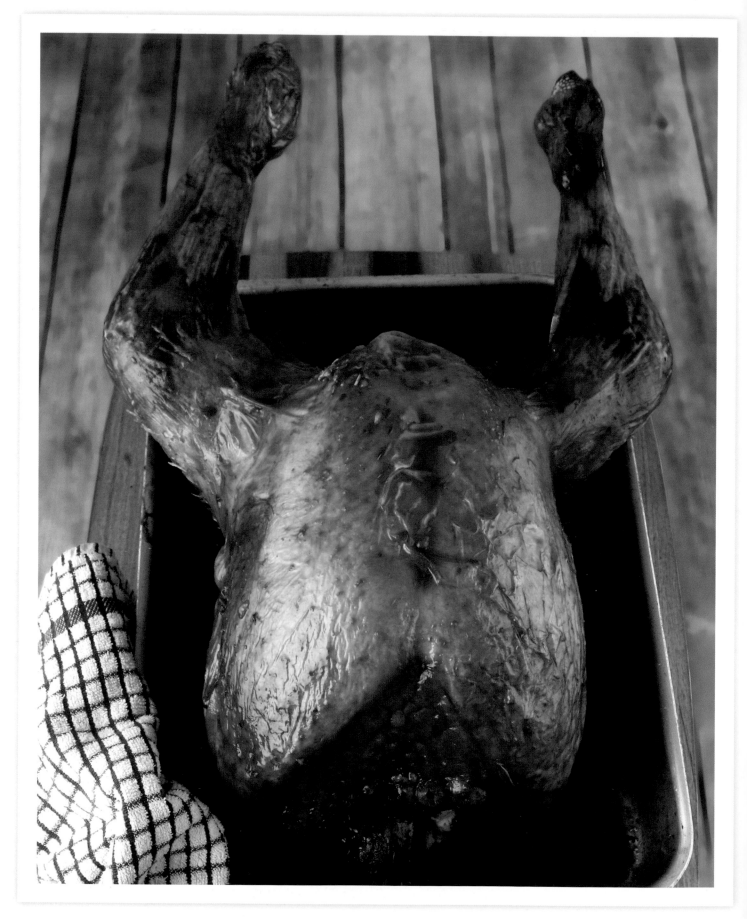

# CHRISTMAS ROAST TURKEY

Christmas dinner is my favorite meal of the year to cook. A lot of people get stressed about it as getting the timing right can be really difficult. This recipe will help you get it right this year and ensure everything runs smoothly on the day. Below is a chart with step by step times for 6 different turkey weights. Check the weight of yours, (it will be on the packaging or receipt) then follow the times on the chart for that weight. The cooking time is calculated using a simple formula: cook for 20 minutes at 180°C or gas mark 4, then the rest of the time at 160°C or gas mark 3. The rule with turkey is 20 minutes per 500g, plus 20 minutes extra. Rest it for 15-30 minutes before you carve. I love to create a nice rub to on my turkey before roasting it which adds a great flavour.

**This is for a 2.5kg/5.5lb bird**
### INGREDIENTS
- 1 tbsp paprika
- 2 tsp salt
- 2 tsp white pepper
- 4 tbsp olive oil

### METHOD
1. Mix together then rub all over the turkey before roasting.

### Roasting the turkey
1. Place the turkey in a roasting tin, cover with foil and follow the chart below to suit the weight.

2. Remove the foil just before you baste for the first time. Basting involves spooning the turkey's juices over it during cooking to keep it moist. Removing the foil will allow the skin to go brown and crispy during the last stage of cooking.

3. Resting meat is very important - rest a small bird for 15 minutes and a larger bird for 30 minutes. Loosely cover with foil to help keep it warm.

4. I don't recommend stuffing a turkey if you are an inexperienced cook and the chart below isn't for a stuffed turkey. If you do stuff yours, ensure the stuffing is piping hot in the centre.

5. To check if your turkey is cooked, pierce the thickest part between the breast and the leg with a knife or skewer.

6. The juices must run clear with no trace of any pink or blood. If not, then pop back into the oven for 15 minutes or so then test again.

7. I strongly advise getting a food thermometer as it is the best and easiest way to tell if your food is thoroughly cooked. Check in a few spots to ensure the temperature is 75°C or above all over.

## Roast Turkey Cooking Times – follow this guideline for your turkey to be ready at 2pm

| Weight | 1kg/2.2lb | 1.5kg/3.3lb | 2kg/4.4lb | 2.5kg/5.5lb | 5kg/11lb | 7.5kg/16.5lb |
|---|---|---|---|---|---|---|
| Pre-Heat Oven | 12:20 | 12:00 | 11:30 | 11:10 | 09:30 | 07:50 |
| 200c, 180c Fan, GM6 | 12.45 | 12:20 | 11:50 | 11:30 | 09:50 | 08:10 |
| 180c, 160c Fan, GM4 | 12.45 | 12:20 | 11:50 | 11:30 | 09:50 | 08:10 |
| Baste, Remove Foil | 13:25 | 13:15 | 13:10 | 12:50 | 12:10 | 09:30 |
| Baste | | | | | 13:10 | 10:30 |
| Baste | | | | | | 11:30 |
| Baste | | | | | | 12:30 |
| Remove & Rest | 13:45 | 13:45 | 13:30 | 13:30 | 13:30 | 13:30 |
| Carve | 14:00 | 14:00 | 14:00 | 14:00 | 14:00 | 14:00 |

Christmas morning can be hectic, especially if you have kids or family coming to stay. Having to cope with dinner for a pile of people on top of everything else can be stressful. This recipe will show you how to make life a lot easier by preparing your turkey and ham in advance. It gets two of the biggest jobs out of the way and eases some of the stress.

**Prep time 10-15 mins •**
**Cook time 15-20 mins**

- **Roast your turkey as per page 134**
- **Boil then glaze your ham as per page 215**
- **Make your stuffing as per page 196**

## METHOD

**1.** Allow the turkey and ham to cool then carve even slices from each.

**2.** Lay a nice sized slice of ham on a baking tray or roasting tin, top this with a ball of stuffing then some of the brown turkey meat followed by 2 nice slices of turkey. These last two slices should overlap and cover the rest.

**3.** Repeat until you have as many portions put together as you need. Use another roasting tin or baking tray if needed. See my leftover recipes on page 138-141 for some ideas on what to do with any leftovers.

**4.** Using the roasting tins as a guide, cut a piece of baking parchment so it just fits inside the tin then soak it in water.

**5.** Pour about 50ml of water in with the turkey and ham portions, cover with the baking parchment then cover the whole tin with tin foil. Store in the fridge until needed.

**6.** To re-heat, pre-heat your oven to 180°C or gas mark 4.

**7.** Place the roasting tins or baking trays in and leave for 15–20 minutes. Dish up all the vegetables and spuds as you normally do for Christmas.

**8.** Remove the trays from the oven and then carefully remove the foil and parchment. You now have beautifully moist and perfectly portioned turkey and ham ready to serve.

# NO-HASSLE TURKEY AND HAM

# TURKEY LEFTOVERS

Most people are well sick of turkey after Christmas. Why not make leftovers a lot more interesting so you and your family can enjoy them this year? I have included 2 simple recipes. Let your imagination run wild and come up with your own creations. See my sauce section from page 202 to get some inspiration.

## *Leftover bake*

You don't have to wait until you have leftovers to make this great dish. You could even pop a chicken in the oven to roast or use fresh chicken breasts if you aren't using turkey. The crumb on this dish makes it extra tasty and gives it a lovely texture.

**Prep time 20 mins** ● **Cook time 35 mins** ● **Serves 4-6**

### INGREDIENTS

**The filling**
- **300–400g cooked turkey meat**
- **1 onion, finely chopped**
- **1 garlic clove, finely chopped**
- **2 peppers, 1 slice removed for the topping**
- **250ml fresh cream**
- **¼ vegetable or chicken stock cube**
- **Hint of black pepper**
**The crumb**
- **3-5 slices of white bread or 200g-300g fresh breadcrumbs**
- **½ red or white onion**
- **1 garlic clove**
- **10–15 fresh basil leaves or ½ tsp dried oregano**
- **150g cheddar cheese, grated**
- **100g ham (optional)**
- **Hint of black pepper**

### METHOD

**1.** Chop the pepper into medium cubes. If you have large slices of turkey you can cut them into bite-sized cubes.

**2.** Heat the oil in a pan then add the onion and garlic and cook for 2 minutes without colouring.

**3.** Add the peppers, cook for another minute then add the turkey, cream, a touch of black pepper and stock cube.

**4.** Heat until it boils and just starts to thicken. Don't stir it too much or you will break the turkey up. Check the seasoning and add more pepper or salt as needed.

**5.** Add all the crumb ingredients into a blender or food processor and blitz.

**6.** Pour the sauce and turkey into a medium sized casserole dish, but don't overfill it or it will overflow when you add the crumb and bake it.

**7.** Place your dish on a baking tray to save your oven from drips while it's cooking. Spread the crumb topping over the top of the bake and cook for 25-30 minutes.

■ ***Tastes great served on its own or with a nice salad.***

## *Vegetarian alternative*

*Leave the turkey out and add more peppers, peas and spinach leaves to make a great vegetarian bake with a tasty, crunchy crust.*

# Turkey Noodles

I use black beans in this though if you don't like them you can leave them out. The main point of this recipe is to help inspire you to come up with your own creations to make those leftovers more interesting.

**Prep time 15 mins** • **Cook time 10 mins** • **Serves 4**

## INGREDIENTS
- 500g medium egg noodles
- 1 onion
- 1 garlic clove, chopped
- 150g mange tout or 100g French beans (optional)
- 1 pepper
- ½ inch piece of ginger, chopped
- 1 tbsp soy sauce
- 3 tbsp oyster sauce or sweet chilli (don't use black beans if using sweet chilli)
- 1 tbsp fermented black beans
- 2 tsp fish sauce
- 25ml water
- 2 tbsp sesame or vegetable oil

## METHOD
**1.** Cook the noodles as per the instructions on the packet, drain and cool under a running cold tap. Set to one side.

**2.** Chop the onion and pepper into medium sized chunks. Cut the onion in half then each half into quarters then the cut the pepper a similar size.

**3.** Heat the oil in a wok or deep pan, add the garlic, ginger, peppers, mange tout, onions and French beans if using them. Cook for 2 minutes on a high heat, ensuring you keep the food moving all the time.

**4.** Add the fish sauce, soy sauce, oyster sauce and the water. Stir well then add the black beans if using them.

**5.** Stir really well then add the turkey and give it a gentle stir. Leave to simmer for 1 minute before adding the noodles. Gently stir once more, taste and serve.

# TURKEY BURGERS

These make a really tasty and healthy alternative to beef burgers. These yummy turkey burgers are made with a bit of a twist.

**Prep time 10 mins** •
**Cook time 20 mins** •
**Serves 6**

## INGREDIENTS
- 450g minced turkey
- 1 slice of red pepper, diced
- 1 tsp oyster sauce
- 1 tsp light soy sauce
- 1 tsp fish sauce
- Small bunch of fresh coriander, chopped
- 1 slice of red pepper
- ¼ fresh chilli, finely chopped
- ½ inch piece of fresh ginger, chopped
- 2 tbsp olive oil
- 6 burger baps
- Lettuce leaves
- Mayonnaise and sweet chilli sauce to top

## METHOD
**1.** Mix all the burger ingredients - apart from the buns, lettuce, mayonnaise, olive oil and sweet chilli sauce - in a bowl, divide into 6 pieces. Then, using your hands, shape it into a burger.
**2.** Heat 2 tbsp of oil in a pan then cook the burgers until browned - about 1 minute each on side.
**3.** Place burgers on a baking tray and pop in the oven for 15–20 minutes. Ensure they are fully cooked by cutting into one or use a food thermometer, they must be 75°C or above.
**4.** Mix the mayonnaise and sweet chilli sauce together in a cup or bowl. Spread some on each bun then add the burger and lettuce followed by the top of the bun.

*Liam's tip*
This burger is also great with a good curry sauce. I love it with Thai green curry.

*Recipe notes*

# Recipe notes

FISH/
SHELLFISH

# SAM'S SEAFOOD
## ATHLONE'S QUALITY FISHMONGER

**Phone (090) 647 2901
or find him on Facebook**

■ Sam is a great guy who is as passionate about fish as I am about cooking it. He has been a huge supporter of BiaMaith from the beginning and gave me fish when I had nothing to cook for the page. He was one of the first suppliers I approached about being part of this book - it was a no brainer for me, especially since Sam knows all there is to know about good fish. He's always ready with tips on everything from choosing the best cuts to barbecuing. I adore seafood of all sorts. Whether it's crab, prawns, a bit of smoked salmon or fresh hake - it's so versatile and quick to cook. And of course it's really healthy as well, which is a huge benefit.

Fish isn't known for being a budget option, but it doesn't have to be expensive either. You can shop special offers and a little goes a long way when you're making things like chowder or fish pie.

The recipes in this book containing fish will mean you can easily introduce it in your weekly meal plans. Sam's Seafood can be found at Scotchparade in Athlone, Co. Westmeath.

# THAI GARLIC AND CHILLI PRAWNS

This is my take on prawns pil pil. It's a healthy dish that is really quick to make and it tastes fantastic. I recommend serving it with crusty bread and a delicious green salad.

### Prep time 10 mins • Cook time 10 mins • Serves 4

## INGREDIENTS

- 24 raw king prawns, peeled and deveined
- 1 red or green chilli or half of each, thinly sliced (keep the seeds in if you want it extra spicy)
- 2 garlic cloves, very thinly sliced
- 16 cherry tomatoes
- 5 tbsp olive oil
- ½ inch fresh ginger, chopped
- Small bunch of fresh coriander, chopped
- Zest of ½ a lime

## METHOD

1. Heat the oil on a pan, then add the garlic and chilli and cook for 1 minute without colouring.
2. Add the tomatoes, ginger and lime zest then cook for another minute.
3. Add the prawns and cook for about 2-3 minutes, until they turn pink.
4. Add the coriander, stir and serve.

# SEAFOOD LASAGNE

Most people are familiar with beef lasagne, but seafood lasagne is something I rarely see on menus. It's a pity because it's such a lovely dish. I have kept this recipe really simple and I use a seafood mix, which makes it a lot cheaper. This is a great way of getting the kids to eat some healthy fish.

**Prep time 20 mins** •
**Cook time 40 mins** • **Serves 6**

## INGREDIENTS

- 500g seafood mix
- 10–15 lasagne sheets
- 1 onion, chopped
- 2 garlic cloves, chopped
- 20 fresh basil leaves
- 500g tomato passata
- 400ml milk
- 1 fish stock cube
- ½ vegetable stock cube
- 120g cheddar cheese, grated
- 1 courgette, diced really small
- 1 large carrot, diced really small
- 2 tbsp olive oil
- 25g flour
- 3 tbsp crème fraiche
- ¼ tsp freshly ground black pepper
- 2 tsp sugar

### Liam's tip

*This goes really well with a light salad as the dish itself is hearty. It also freezes really well. Allow to cool then cut into portions, wrap each with cling film and freeze.*

## METHOD

**1.** Place the milk and vegetable stock cube in a saucepan and slowly bring to the boil.
**2.** Melt the butter in another saucepan then add the flour and stir while cooking for about 1 minute to make a roux.
**3.** Add the roux to the milk and whisk really well; if it is too thick, add a little more milk. Add half the cheese to the sauce, whisk well then set to one side.
**4.** Pre-heat your oven to 180°C or gas mark 4.
**5.** Heat the oil in a pan then add the onion, carrot and garlic. Cook without colouring for 2 minutes, then add the tomato passata, courgette, sugar and pepper. Stir and simmer for 10 minutes.
**6.** Place a layer of fish on the bottom of a dish, then spoon some tomato sauce over it. Cover this with a layer of lasagne sheets. Try not to overlap them - break the sheets to fit if you have to.
**7.** Repeat this until you're left with a layer of lasagne sheets on the top. Spoon a thick layer of cheese sauce over this, then sprinkle with the remainder of the grated cheese.
**9.** Bake for around 40 minutes.

# HERB CRUSTED SALMON

This is such a simple and tasty dish to make. The crust adds so much flavour and texture to the fish. I served it with Gratin Potatoes from page 186 though it would go just as well with a salad, such as the basic Caesar salad from page 46. I'd leave the croutons out as the herb crust will do the job instead.

**Prep time 15 mins ● Cook time 15 mins ● Serves 4**

## INGREDIENTS

**The fish**
- 4 x 150g salmon darnes

**The herb crust**
- 3 slices of white bread
- Small handful of fresh parsley
- 10 basil leaves
- ¼ red pepper
- Zest of ¼ lime
- Pinch of salt and freshly ground pepper

**The sauce**
- 250ml fresh cream
- 5 basil leaves
- 3 spring onions
- 35ml fish stock or a small corner off a fish stock cube
- Freshly ground black pepper
- 1 tbsp olive oil

## METHOD

1. Pre-heat oven to 180°C or gas mark 4. If you plan to serve with gratin potatoes, as shown in the picture, they need to be in the oven 20 minutes before the salmon.

2. Lightly grease a baking tray with a drop of olive oil. Place the salmon on the tray, skin side down.

3. Add all the crumb ingredients to a food processor and blend to a fine crumb. If it's a little wet, spread it out on a baking tray and pop it in the oven for 2 minutes.

4. Spoon this on top of each salmon darne. Don't use sparingly as you'll want a nice coating of about 2cm thick. Bake this in the oven for 15-20 minutes.

5. Just before the salmon is cooked, put the cream in a pan, add the stock cube, pepper, chopped spring onion and basil leaves. Heat until it has reduced and thickened.

6. Taste to ensure you are happy with the seasoning. The spring onions will have a slight bite to them.

7. Remove the salmon from the oven, check to make sure it is cooked.

■ *Serve with the sauce and potatoes or a salad.*

# HAKE FILLET WITH WARM SALAD OF CHERRY TOMATOES, BASIL AND CHORIZO

I'm a big fan of fish, especially hake as it's so versatile. This simple dish will impress your friends and family with very little effort on your part. Add baby new potatoes if you want a heartier dinner.

**Prep time 10 mins • Cook time 15 mins • Serves 2**

## INGREDIENTS

- 2 thick hake fillets, about 175g each
- 16 cherry tomatoes, halved
- 75g chorizo, chopped
- 1 garlic clove, chopped
- 15 fresh basil leaves
- 1 garlic clove
- 4 tbsp olive oil
- Pinch of freshly ground black pepper
- 1 tbsp balsamic vinegar

## METHOD

**1.** Heat 1 tbsp of olive oil in a pan. If the fish's skin is still on, place them skin side down on the pan. If not, then place the opposite side down first.
**2.** Cook for 2-3 minutes, then add the butter and cook for 1 more minute until the skin is nice and crispy.
**3.** Turn the fish, then cook on the other side for 3-4 minutes. The time will depend on how thick the fillets are. Remove from the pan when cooked and leave to rest on a plate.
**4.** Heat the rest of the oil in a clean pan then add the garlic, chorizo and cherry tomatoes. Cook for 2 minutes until the skin starts to fall off the tomatoes.
**5.** Drizzle with the balsamic vinegar and stir, then add the basil leaves and a sprinkling of pepper.

■ *Serve with the warmed chorizo and tomato mix on a plate underneath the hake.*

# SWEET AND SOUR PRAWNS IN CRISPY BATTER

Forget going to a take away and paying a fortune for dishes like this that can easily be made at home. It's way cheaper and much better for you and your family to make something like this from scratch.

**Prep time 15 mins ● Cook time 15 mins ● Serves 4**

## INGREDIENTS
- **24 king prawns, peeled and deveined**
- **30g cornflour**
  The batter
- **225g plain flour**
- **50g cornflour**
- **300ml ice cold soda water or sparkling water (tap water will do)**
  The sauce
- **250ml pineapple juice or water**
- **2 tbsp sugar (8 if using water)**
- **2 tbsp white vinegar**
- **4 tbsp tomato ketchup**
- **2 tbsp cornflour**

## METHOD
### The batter
**1.** Turn your deep fat fryer on to 170°C.
**2.** Mix all the batter ingredients together in a bowl. I use a hand blender to speed it up.

### The sauce
**1.** Add all the sauce ingredients, except the cornflour, to a pot and bring to the boil. Reduce heat, then simmer for 10 minutes.
**2.** Mix the cornflour with 1 tsp of water to form a paste. Whisk the paste into the sauce and bring back to the boil.
Remove from the heat and leave to one side.

### Putting it all together
**1.** Roll the prawns in the cornflour. One by one, dip each prawn into the batter mix, then slowly drop into the fryer.
**2.** Cook for about 2-3 minutes. The prawns will float to the top of the basket when cooked.
**3.** They may stick to the basket so the best way to avoid this is to ensure the basket is lowered before adding the prawns.
■ *Serve with boiled rice and the sauce on the side.*

# SEAFOOD PASTA

I've seen this sold in restaurants for crazy money. Now you can make it at home for a few euro and with little time, skills or effort.

**Prep time 10 mins •**
**Cook time 10 mins •**
**Serves 4**

## INGREDIENTS
- 400g spaghetti or linguine
- 250g seafood mix or 1 small tin tuna or salmon, drained, or 200g smoked salmon
- Napoletana Sauce from page 208
- 1 tbsp lemon juice
- 50g parmesan, grated
- 1 tbsp olive oil
- freshly ground black pepper

## METHOD
1. Cook the pasta as per the instructions on the packet, or make your own. When cooked, cool down under running cold water and drain. Mix in 1 tbsp of olive oil and set to one side.
2. Half fill the pot you cooked the pasta in with hot water then put back on to boil.
3. Pop the Napoletana Sauce in a pot then add the fish and lemon juice. Heat through and ensure the fish is cooked.
4. Place the pasta into the pot of water for 1 minute then drain.
5. Add the pasta and cheese to the sauce and mix gently.
6. Sprinkle some freshly ground pepper over the top then taste and serve.

# HOW TO MAKE BASIC PASTA

If you haven't tried to make your own pasta, then you really should give it a go. All the kneading can be hard work but overall it's easy to get right and is well worth the effort as nothing else comes close to a good homemade pasta. I have never had any packet pasta, fresh, or dried that compares to homemade pasta. Making your own won't save you money, however. In fact, it can be a bit more costly due to all the eggs. If you don't have a machine then you can still make it using a good rolling pin. Try making lasagne sheets to start, then progress onto tagliatelle then other smaller pastas.

**Prep time 1 hour 30 mins • Cook time 3 mins • Serves 4**

## INGREDIENTS
- 6 medium eggs
- 500g 00 flour
- Handful of semolina (optional)
  If you can't find 00 flour use:
- 250g strong white flour
- 250g plain flour
- Drop of oil

## METHOD
1. Sieve the flour onto a clean work surface or into a bowl, then make a well in the centre.
2. Break the eggs into the well and beat using a fork.
3. Using your hands, slowly mix the flour in until it is all mixed and you have a ball of dough.
4. This following step is hard work but it's essential as you need to work the gluten in the flour which gives a lovely smooth pasta. Hold the piece of dough and stretch it out away from you with your other hand, then pull it back and make a ball, repeat again and again until the dough starts to spring back. Once the pasta is nice and smooth, wrap it really well in cling film and leave in the fridge for about 45 minutes.
5. Cut the dough in two. Press down on one piece to get it as flat as possible. Feed this through your pasta machine on the thickest setting. Do this about 3 times then reduce the setting by 1. Repeat, then drop the setting again, only this time roll it through once, then repeat until you get to the 2nd last setting. If the pasta starts to break up then roll back into a ball and start again. You can use a little semolina if it starts to stick - just sprinkle it on the dough as needed.
6. Change the handle to the cutting piece at the back of the machine then start to feed the pasta through. If it doesn't cut properly your dough may be too soft. Roll it into a ball then put it through the pasta machine again. You may need to sprinkle a little semolina to stop it sticking when you feed it through the cutter.
7. You can either allow it to dry in portions or cook it there and then. Boil some salted water with a tiny dash of oil then add the pasta and boil for 2-3 minutes. Drain and serve with your favourite sauce.

# SMOKED SALMON PASTA

I really enjoy this dish and it's so simple to make. You seriously need zero cooking skills to master it and you'll get restaurant-quality results every time. Just take your time and read the recipe before starting.

**Prep time 10 mins •
Cook time 10 mins • Serves 4**

## INGREDIENTS
- 250ml fresh cream
- 400g spaghetti or linguine
- 250g smoked salmon
- 10 chives
- 1 small onion, chopped, or shallot, finely chopped or leave the chives and onion out and use 4 chopped spring onions instead
- 2 tbsp olive oil
- 50ml white wine

## METHOD
**1.** Cook the pasta as per the instructions on the packet or make your own. When cooked, cool down under running cold water and drain. Mix in 1 tbsp of olive oil and set to one side.

**2.** Half fill the pot you cooked the pasta in with hot water then place back on to boil.

**3** Heat remaining oil in a pan then add the onion, shallot or spring onion. Cook for 1 minute.

**4.** Add the white wine and boil until about half has evaporated.

**5.** Add the cream and reduce until it starts to thicken, then slice the smoked salmon and chives and add them in.

**6.** Heat the pasta by placing it back in the boiling water for 1 minute. Drain then add to the sauce with the black pepper.

**7.** Stir gently then taste. Adjust seasoning if necessary and serve.

# Recipe notes

# Recipe notes

VEGETARIAN

# PENNE ARRABIATA

This simple, cheap, and quick spicy Italian classic is great as a dinner or lunch. Serve it with crusty bread oozing with melted garlic butter.

**Prep time 10 mins** ●
**Cook time 10 mins** ●
**Serves 4**

## INGREDIENTS
- 400g penne pasta
- 1 x 400g tin chopped tomatoes or 500g tomato passata
- 1 red chilli, chopped
- 2 garlic cloves, chopped
- 1 tsp sugar
- 1 small onion, chopped
- 10-15 fresh basil leaves
- 3 tbsp olive oil

## METHOD
**1.** Cook the penne as per the instructions on the packet in boiling, salted water with 1 tbsp of oil added. When cooked, drain in a colander and cool under cold, running water.
**2.** Heat the remaining olive oil in a pan then add the onion, chilli and garlic for 3–4 minutes. The onions should be soft and translucent, but not coloured.
**3.** Add the chopped tomatoes or passata and sugar, then stir and leave to simmer for 10 minutes.
**4.** Add the fresh basil leaves then the drained pasta. Stir well, then taste and adjust seasoning before serving.

# VEGAN VEGGIE LASAGNE

Lasagne is great - it's easy to make and tastes fantastic. I'm not a vegetarian but would happily munch away on a mushroom lasagne and think myself well fed and satisfied afterwards. My veggie lasagne takes a little more work but I think it is worth the effort. I really hope you enjoy it as much as my friends and recipe testers did.

**Prep time 30 mins ● Cook time 1 hour ● Serves 4-6**

## INGREDIENTS

- 2 aubergines
- 3 courgettes
- 3 peppers
- 50g pine nuts
- 4 garlic cloves
- ½ vegan/vegetable stock cube
- 300ml water
- 25g flour
- 25g non-dairy spread
- 10-12 lasagne sheets
- 15-20 fresh basil leaves
- 6 big tomatoes
- 6 tbsp olive oil
- 100g vegan cheese, grated as best you can or roasted butternut squash puree*

*Cut a butternut squash in half and scoop out the seeds. Roast half of it in the oven for around 15-20 minutes at 180°C .
When cooked, scoop out the flesh, mash or puree it, then season with some salt and pepper and a hint of freshly grated nutmeg.

## METHOD

1. Pre-heat your oven to 180°C or gas mark 4.
2. Line a baking tray with tin foil. Lay the peppers on it and pop it in the oven and bake for 20 minutes. Remove from the oven, turn and cook for another 15 minutes. Remove from the oven and allow to cool.
3. Cut the aubergines in thin slices and place in a bowl with 4 unpeeled cloves of garlic. Add 2 tbsp of olive oil and a sprinkling of freshly ground black pepper and a pinch of salt. Gently mix to coat the garlic and aubergine.
4. Lay each slice down on a roasting tin or baking tray then place in the oven and roast for about 8 minutes. Keep doing batches if you have to. You will need the bowl again soon so don't wash it.
5. Meanwhile, slice the tomatoes so that they're about 2cm thick.
6. Remove the aubergine and garlic from the oven. Peel the garlic and place this and half of the aubergine and all of the pine nuts in a food processor. Blitz for about 30 seconds, so that it still has a bit of texture. Set to one side.
7. Slice the courgettes into thick slices the pop them into the bowl you had the aubergines and garlic in earlier. Add a pinch of salt and pepper and mix gently.
8. Pour the water in a pot add ½ a stock cube and bring back to the boil.
9. Meanwhile, melt the vegan spread in the microwave. When ready mix in the flour to form a paste. This is an easy vegan roux.
10. When the water has boiled add ½ the roux and whisk really well. It will thicken, you want it nice and thick so it coats the back of a spoon. Add more roux and whisk briskly again if it isn't thick enough.
11. Place a layer of aubergines on the bottom of a medium casserole or pie dish. Top this with a layer of roasted peppers then a layer of tomatoes followed by a sprinkling of chopped basil leaves.
12. Spread a good dollop of the aubergine paste over 3 or 4 lasagne sheets then place them paste side down on top of the veggies in the dish.
13. Spread a layer of courgette on top then another layer of tomatoes, followed by a sprinkling of fresh basil and a dash of salt and pepper.
14. Pour a good ladle of sauce on top then top with a layer of lasagne.
15. Repeat this until you run out of ingredients or room in the dish. The last layer should be lasagne sheets topped with butternut squash topping or sauce and grated cheese topping.
16. Spread the butternut squash puree on top then bake in the oven for 20-25 minutes.

# FUSILLI WITH ROASTED PEPPER AND CHILLI RELISH

This is such a simple yet really tasty pasta dish. It's great for those nights you want something satisfying but don't have a lot of time.

**Prep time 2 mins • Cook time 10 mins • Serves 4**

## INGREDIENTS
- **400g fusilli pasta**
- **25g butter**
- **75g Roasted Red Pepper and Chilli Relish page 207**
- **Pinch of freshly ground black pepper**
- **15g parmesan cheese to taste**

## METHOD
**1.** Cook the pasta as per the instructions on the packet, usually around 8 minutes. Ensure you add a good bit of salt to the water.

**2.** When the pasta is cooked, remove from the heat, drain the water then run under a cold tap until it is cold. This washes the starch off.

**3.** Fill the pot with water and place it on to boil. When it's ready pop the pasta back in again for around a minute.

**4.** Remove and drain again only don't cool it down this time.

**5.** Melt the butter in a pan and add the relish.

**6.** Add the pasta and give it a good stir.

**7.** Grate a little parmesan in, followed by a few twists of a black pepper mill. Mix well, taste to check the seasoning and serve.

### Liam's tip
*To check if dried pasta is cooked, remove a piece from the water and cut into it. If uncooked, it will have a creamy white bit in the middle which disappears when fully cooked. Always serve pasta with a slight bite to it and never mushy.*

# Recipe notes

*Recipe notes*

SIDES

# HOW TO COOK BROCCOLI

Broccoli is a superfood and is an amazing vegetable that has so many health benefits for you and your family. I'm not going to go into the science of it here only to say that it is something that should be on your weekly menu plan. It helps fight cancer, helps prevent aging, is great for hair and skin, gives energy, keeps bones healthy and loads more.

### Storing

Store broccoli in the vegetable compartment at the bottom of your fridge. Keep it in a bag but don't seal the bag. You could also make a few holes in the side. The younger and fresher the broccoli, the better. It can have a bitter taste if old or not stored correctly.

### Cooking

So many people overcook broccoli to the point where it's mush and tastes horrible. Broccoli should have a bite to it rather than be totally soft.

In a pot, bring water and 1 tsp salt to the boil and add the broccoli. There should be enough water to cover it. Bring back to the boil and continue to boil for 1–2 minutes, depending on how big you've cut the florets. Don't try cooking really big florets as the top will turn to mush before the stalk is cooked. Remove a piece using a spoon or fork then gently press the stalk. It should be slightly soft though not too soft. If it's still really hard return it to the water for another minute. When cooked, place in ice cold water to cool down, drain and serve immediately.

### Broccoli Hollandaise

Follow my recipe for hollandaise sauce on page 211 then simply pour over your cooked broccoli for a seriously tasty veggie dish.

# THE PERFECT MASH

You can't beat a bit of mashed potato with a dinner. It's my favourite way to eat a spud, especially with any wet dish like stew, or alongside a big slice of roast beef, vegetables and gravy. It's also delicious with a thick juicy steak with loads of pepper sauce. This recipe will show you how to make the perfect mash. I bet your friends or family tell you it's the best mash they have ever eaten.

**Prep time 10 mins ● Cook time 10-15 mins ● Serves 2-4**

## INGREDIENTS
- **8 good sized rooster or maris pipers**
- **25-50ml fresh cream**
- **50g butter**
- **Pinch of white pepper and salt to taste.**

## METHOD
**1.** Half fill a medium pot with water and place on the boil. You will need a steam attachment for it, or a colander that sits on top.
**2.** Peel the potatoes, or simply wash them if you're keeping the skins on, I prefer to steam them in their jackets.
**3.** Place the potatoes in the steamer or colander, then cover with the lid or tin foil. Pierce a hole in the foil if using it.
**4.** Bring the water to the boil and keep at a rolling boil for 15 minutes or so.

Test the spuds with a fork - if it goes through easily without any resistance they are cooked.
**5.** Remove the skins whilst holding the potatoes with a clean tea towel. Be careful not to burn your fingers.
**6.** Place a mouli sieve (see pic) on top of a bowl or pot then pass the potatoes through. If you don't have one then use a potato ricer or a simple masher.
**7.** Add the butter and cream to a pot or non-stick pan and allow the butter to melt at medium heat. Add the mashed potatoes and a pinch of salt and white pepper.
**8.** Stir well as you keep them on the heat. They will start to come together in one creamy lump.
**9.** Taste and add more salt and pepper to suit you preference.

## *Variations*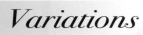

Some people call mash infused with cabbage colcannon, and others, like my mum, call it champ. To me, colcannon is mash infused with spring onion. Either way it's delicious - especially with loads of real butter through it.

### ■ COLCANNON
Add 4 chopped, raw spring onions to the mash when you add the butter and cream, then follow the basic recipe.

### ■ BACON AND CHEESE MASH
I used to serve a lot of this with steaks when I had it on menus. It was extremely popular - so much so that we easily sold 4 times more of this mash than any other variety on offer.
Fry 4 smoked rashers until they are really crispy but not burnt. Allow them to cool, then either chop them up or pop them into a food processor and pulse for 20 seconds. Add the bacon bits you just made along with 100g mature white cheddar cheese, or even a nice brie, chopped into small pieces. Mix both into the mash immediately after you add it to the cream and butter. Follow the rest of the basic recipe.

### ■ HORSERADISH MASH

This is awesome with roast beef. It has a lovely kick to it which people won't be expecting. I love watching their faces as they take the first bite and realise the wonderful new flavours they weren't expecting.
Add 1-2 tbsp of horseradish sauce from a jar. Do this when the mash has been mixed in the pot just before you serve it.

### ■ CHAMP

This is really good on its own with a few fried rashers or a thick slice of cooked ham or bacon.
Chop 75g fresh cabbage up really finely. Add to the pan when you add the butter then add 1 tsp of olive oil to stop the butter from burning. Cook for 2 minutes then add the cream and cook for 1 more minute. Then add the mash and seasoning and finish as per the basic recipe.

### ■ GARLIC MASH

Try this with roast chicken or as a topping on a rich seafood pie.
Finely chop 2 garlic cloves then add to the butter and allow the flavour to infuse into the butter.
Then follow the recipe as normal.
You can also use wild garlic alongside the garlic cloves.
Use 1 clove instead of 2 then a small handful of chopped wild garlic.

# GRATIN POTATOES

**Liam's tip**

*To make slicing a potato easier, cut a sliver off one side of the potato so it lays flat and stable, this will help you cut even slices. Don't worry if you can't get them too thin, the main thing is all the slices are as even as possible. .*

**Prep time 15 mins ● Cook time 40 mins ● Serves 4-6**

## INGREDIENTS

- 200ml cream
- 3 garlic cloves, finely chopped
- ½ tsp freshly ground black pepper
- 100g white cheddar cheese, grated
- 8–10 large potatoes
- 2 onions, very thinly sliced (optional)

## METHOD

**1.** Pre-heat your oven to 180°C or gas mark 4.

**2.** Put the cream, garlic and pepper in a pot then place on a low heat.

**3.** Peel all the potatoes then slice them as thinly as possible. (See tip)

**4.** Place a layer of the sliced potatoes in the bottom of a casserole dish. Add a layer of very thinly sliced onions if using them.

**5.** Sprinkle over a little pepper and salt then a little cheese.

**6.** Repeat steps 4 and 5 until you have used all the potatoes.

**7.** Pour the cream over the top slowly so as to allow it soak through and not overflow.

**8.** Cover the casserole dish with tin foil then place it in the middle of your oven for 30 minutes.

**9.** Remove from the oven, remove the foil then cook in the oven for 10 more minutes.

**11.** Scoop them out with a serving spoon or allow to cool slightly then use a cake cutter or fish slice to cut and lift a portion out.

# MUSHROOM AND SHALLOT RAGOUT

These make an awesome base for some vegetarian dishes, though they go just as well with a steak, lamb, chicken or even a burger. Look for wild mushrooms like oyster, shitake, chestnut, etc. If you can't get wild, then just use regular button and chestnut like I used. The dish can be served as a side or on crunchy toast. Or simply add some lovely fresh egg pasta and top with fresh parmesan cheese.

**Prep time 10 mins • Cooking time 15 mins • Serves 4**

## METHOD

- **450g mixed button and chestnut mushrooms**
- **12 shallots, peeled**
- **2 tsp paprika**
- **75ml red wine**
- **15 basil leaves**
- **½ tsp freshly ground black pepper**
- **¼ tsp salt**
- **2 tsp Dijon mustard**
- **30g butter**
- **1 tbsp olive oil**

## METHOD

**1.** Heat the butter and olive oil in a deep pan or pot, ideally something with a lid.

**2.** Add the shallots, cover and leave on a low heat for 5 minutes.

**3.** Add the mushrooms, give them a good stir then cover again and leave for 5 minutes more.

**4.** Add the paprika, pepper and salt then stir well before adding the red wine. Cover for 2 minutes more.

**5.** Add the mustard, stir well and finally cover for 2 more minutes before serving.

# GREEN VEGETABLES WITH RED PEPPER & BASIL BUTTER

I'm a massive fan of a healthy plate of green veggies. I could sit and eat them on their own, although I'd much prefer then as a side with a nice big juicy steak or a roast dinner. I've added a simple yet tasty butter to give them some colour and extra flavour plus it makes them look so much better in a serving bowl or plate.

The most important part of this recipe is timing. Cooking vegetables properly can be hard to get right and it's easy to end up with over-cooked or under-cooked veg. Follow this recipe and you will end up with perfectly cooked vegetables every time.

**Prep time 5-10 mins ● Cook time 12 mins ● Serves 4**

## INGREDIENTS

- 100g French beans, fresh or frozen
- 100g mange tout
- 100g frozen peas (I prefer petit pois)
- 200g broccoli
- 75g butter
- 1 garlic clove
- 1 red pepper
- 10 basil leaves
- ¼ chilli (optional)
- ½ vegetable stock cube (optional)
- 1 tsp olive oil

## METHOD

**1.** Top and tail the French beans (cut the tips off them) then cut the broccoli into bite size florets.

**2.** Put some water on to boil with either 1 tsp of salt or ½ a stock cube.

**3.** Ensure your butter is at room temperature. If it's too hard, soften it in the microwave.

**4.** Peel the garlic, then remove the stalk and seeds from the pepper. Stick all of these plus the basil leaves (and the chilli, if you're using it) into a food processor and blitz until blended. Place in a bowl with the butter, mix well and set to one side.

**5.** Place the French beans into the pot of boiling salted water and cook for 4 minutes. If using frozen beans, skip this step and start cooking them with the broccoli.

### Liam's tip
*The butter tastes really great with fish. Just add 1 tsp of lemon juice when you blend the ingredients.*

**6.** Pop the broccoli in and cook for 1 minute, then add the mange tout and cook for another minute. Throw in the frozen peas and cook for a further 3 minutes.

**7.** Remove from the heat and drain off the water. Fill up the pot with cold water and drain again. Repeat this step until the vegetables are cold. This prevents them from continuing to cook in their own steam.

**8.** Just before you're ready to serve, put another pot of water on to boil but don't add salt this time. Pop the vegetables back into the boiling water (be careful not to splash yourself) and heat up the veg for about 2 minutes. In the meantime, heat a pan with 1 tsp olive oil and 1 tbsp of the butter you made earlier.

**9.** Drain all the water from the vegetables. Place them in the pan and toss for about 1 minute. Add a pinch of freshly ground black pepper and salt.

■ *Serve with the rest of the butter on top or in a little bowl on the side.*

# GIANT ONION RINGS

These are lovely on their own or with a nice steaks, ribs or BBQ chicken. These cost very little to make and are really easy, plus they're much better than the processed frozen variety.

**Prep time 10 mins ● Cook time 5 mins ● Serves 2-4**

## INGREDIENTS
- **1-2 large Spanish onions**
- **75g cornflour**
  **The batter**
- **225g plain flour**
- **50g cornflour**
- **300ml ice-cold soda water or sparkling water (cold tap water will do)**
- **Pinch of salt and white pepper**

## METHOD

**1.** Heat your deep fat fryer to 170°C.

**2.** Add all the batter ingredients to a bowl and whisk well. You could also use a hand blender.

**3.** Take the root and top off the onions then cut into 1 inch thick rings. Remove the skin then push the rings apart. Roll these in the cornflour as it will help the batter stick to them.

**4.** Drop the basket of your fryer in the oil.

**5.** Coat an onion ring into the batter then dip a bit of the onion ring into the oil for about 5-10 seconds before dropping it completely into the basket. This stops it from sticking to the basket. Cook around 2 onion rings at a time so you don't overload the basket and end up having them all stuck together. Turn the onion rings after about 1 minute.

**6.** Let them cook for another minute or two then lift from the fryer onto a plate covered in kitchen paper. Repeat these steps until you've used up all the onion.

**7.** If the first ones seem cold and soggy, simply drop back into the oil for a minute or so. It's OK to pile them in this time as they won't stick.

■ *I love eating these with my Aioli dip which can be found on page 212.*

# HONEY AND ROSEMARY ROASTED CARROTS AND PARSNIPS

These are great with a nice roast dinner. It's time consuming and costly to turn on the oven especially for them otherwise. The rosemary in this goes really well with the sweetness of the honey.

**Prep time 10 mins • Cook time 20-30 mins • Serves 4**

## INGREDIENTS
- 4 large carrots
- 4 parsnips
- 2 tbsp honey
- 2 tbsp olive oil
- 2 fresh rosemary sprigs

## METHOD
**1.** Pre-heat your oven to 180°C or gas mark 4.
**2.** Peel the vegetables, then cut the ends off.
**3.** Cut them into big chunks, as shown in the photo here.
**4.** Place them on a roasting tin or baking tray, add the olive oil and rub it in so it coats each piece. Use more oil if needed.
**5.** Place in the oven for 10 minutes.
**6.** Remove from the oven then cut the rosemary sprigs in 4, place them and the honey on the tray with the vegetables and give them a good stir. Return to the oven for 10 more minutes, or until they start to soften slightly.
**7.** Remove from the oven, stir and serve.

# SAUTÉED CABBAGE WITH SMOKED BACON AND ONION

I think cabbage is underrated. It's so good for you and really does taste great when cooked properly. The problem is so many people - including many chefs - don't know how to do it properly. Once you've tasted this recipe, it'll become one of your favourite ways to eat it.

**Prep time 10 mins ●**
**Cook time 10 mins ● Serves 6**

## INGREDIENTS
- **1 Savoy or York cabbage**
- **2 vegetable stock cubes**
- **200g smoked rashers**
- **1 red onion**
- **35g butter**
- **Pinch of freshly ground black pepper**

## METHOD
**1.** Bring a large pot half filled with water to the boil and add the stock cubes.
**2.** Cut the cabbage in half from the root to the top then cut into quarters.
**3.** Turn a quarter onto its side and chop off the stalk with a sharp knife.
**4.** With the stalk removed, turn the quarter sideways and cut it into thin strips. Do this for each piece.
**5.** Fill your sink or a bowl with water and wash the cabbage. Any grit or soil will sink to the bottom so make sure there is enough water to allow the cabbage to float.
**6.** Remove the cabbage from the water and stick it in the pot. Cover and allow to boil for 5 or 6 minutes.
**7.** Meanwhile, slice the rashers as thinly as possible.
**8.** Heat a pan with about 1 tbsp of olive oil then add the bacon and cook until almost crispy.
**9.** Slice the onion and add to the pan. Cook until they're soft and starting to brown.
**10.** Add the butter, allow to melt then add the cabbage.
**11.** Sauté this on a high heat for 3–5 minutes then add a sprinkling of freshly ground pepper. Adjust seasoning and serve.

*Liam's tip*

*This makes a healthy alternative topping to a chicken and bacon pie, shepherd's pie or with some boiled baby new potatoes with a knob of real butter.*

# CAULIFLOWER CHEESE

I love this dish and believe it or not, I actually prefer it with frozen cauliflower. But you can use fresh or frozen and I bet you'll love it either way. I experiment with different cheeses from time to time, too. A strong brie is great and smoked cheese is fantastic in it, but blue cheese doesn't work with it at all.

**Prep time 10 mins • Cook time 25 mins • Serves 6**

## INGREDIENTS
- 1 bag of frozen cauliflower or 1 head of fresh
- 1 vegetable stock cube
- 250ml fresh milk
- 200g cheddar cheese, grated or you could use 100g of cheddar and 100g of brie
- 50g flour
- 50g butter

## METHOD
1. Pre-heat your oven to 180°C or gas mark 4.
2. If using frozen cauliflower, place in a pot of water, cover, bring to the boil, reduce heat and simmer for 6 minutes. If using fresh cauliflower, cut into florets place into boiling water and boil for 10 minutes. Strain.
3. Add the cooked cauliflower to an oven proof dish.
4. Place the milk into the pot, then slowly bring to the boil adding all of the cheese and the stock cube, stirring all the time. The cheese will thicken the sauce.
5. If the sauce needs to thicken more, melt 50g of butter or margarine in a pot then add 50g of flour. Cook for about 1 minute. Add this to the sauce little by little until it thickens. Allow time for it to do it's work before adding more. It won't thicken until the sauce is close to boiling. If it ends up too thick add a little more milk.
6. Pour the sauce over the cauliflower, then place in the oven for 15-20 minutes until the top is golden brown.

# GARLIC POTATOES

This dish goes so well with many meals and is fairly easy to make. If you don't have baby new or salad potatoes, boil roosters or similar, peel them when cooked and cooled and cut them in quarters.

**Prep time 5 mins •
Cook time 15-30 mins •
Serves 6**

## INGREDIENTS
- 1kg bag of baby new or salad potatoes
- 300ml milk
- 25g flour
- 25g butter or margarine
- 1 vegetable or chicken stock cube
- 4 garlic cloves, chopped
- Small bunch of parsley, chopped

## METHOD
**1.** Pre-heat your oven to 180°C or gas mark 4.
**2.** Place the potatoes into a pot of boiling water ensuring they are completely covered.
**3.** Bring to the boil and turn down to about half heat, leave to cook for 10-15 minutes. Bigger potatoes take longer. Pierce with a fork to test if they are cooked.
**4.** In another pot, add the garlic and butter, melt slowly then add the flour. Stir well, then add the milk, stock cube and chopped parsley. Slowly bring to the boil. Add more milk if it's too thick. Taste to check the seasoning.
**5.** Place the potatoes into an oven-proof dish and pour over the sauce and bake in the oven for 15 minutes.

### Gluten free option
Bring 250ml cream to the boil, add the stock cube, chopped parsley and garlic then reduce to thicken. Pour over the potatoes and either bake in the oven or serve as is.

# SAGE AND ONION STUFFING

I love a good stuffing, be it in a sandwich or with a Sunday roast. This one is very easy and takes just a few minutes.I strongly advise making your own breadcrumbs if you have a blender or food processor as they are a fraction of the price.

**Prep time 10 mins ● Cook time 10 mins ● Serves 6**

## INGREDIENTS
- **8 slices of white sliced bread or 400g breadcrumbs**
- **150g butter**
- **1 large onion, very finely chopped**
- **2 garlic cloves, very finely chopped**
- **5 tsp dried sage**
- **¼ tsp salt**
- **¼ tsp pepper**
- **5 tbsp gravy (optional)**

## METHOD
**1.** If making your own breadcrumbs, tear the bread into small pieces and place in a food processor. Blend 1-2 slices at a time - don't overload it or it won't blend properly.

**2.** Add the butter, onion, dried sage and garlic to a pot and place on a low heat. Allow it to melt and simmer slowly for 3-4 minutes. This releases the flavours into the butter and makes the stuffing nicer.

**3.** Add the salt and pepper, stir, then add the breadcrumbs little by little.

**4.** Remove from the heat and stir until it is mixed well.

**5.** If you aren't stuffing a chicken or cooking it with meat, you can mix some gravy through the stuffing to give it an extra bit of flavour.

### Liam's tip
*Stuffing freezes really well, so why not make a few batches then you can easily defrost some when needed.*

# FRENCH BEANS WITH CRISPY BACON AND WHOLEGRAIN MUSTARD

I sat and ate nearly the whole bowl of these when I made them for the photoshoot for this book. The flavour is amazing. I've even served them to friends as a snack with beer and everyone loved them. The secret is to keep the beans nice and crunchy and the bacon lardons crispy on the outside but juicy on the inside. It's really easy to do.

**Prep time 5 mins • Cook time 6 mins • Serves 2**

## INGREDIENTS
- **250g French beans, with the tops trimmed off them**
- **1 tsp wholegrain mustard**
- **100g smoked bacon lardons, pancetta or smoked rashers**
- **1 tbsp olive oil**
- **1 tbsp butter**
- **1 tsp salt**

## METHOD
1. Add salt to a pot of water and bring to the boil.
2. Add the French beans and cook for 5 minutes.
3. Remove from the heat, drain the water, fill it with cold water then repeat until the beans are cold. This allows you to prepare them in advance and finish when needed.
4. Five minutes before you are ready to serve the French beans put about 250ml of water back in the pot and bring to the boil before adding the beans.
5. Heat 1 tbsp of olive oil in a pan then add the bacon lardons. Cook until they start to turn crispy on the outside.
6. Drain the water from the beans and add them to the pan with the bacon.
7. Add the butter and mustard then toss or stir for about 30 seconds, then serve.

# CREAMY TURNIP WITH FRESH CREAM AND PEPPER

I hated turnips growing up and I'm still not a fan if they are simply boiled. But cooking them like this makes them taste delicious - really sweet and creamy. Try it and I bet your family will love them.

**Prep time 10 mins • Cook time 15-10 mins • Serves 4-6**

## INGREDIENTS
- **1 whole turnip**
- **50ml fresh cream**
- **1 tsp cracked black pepper**
- **25g butter**

## METHOD
1. Cut the turnip in half, root to tip. Lay one half cut side down and starting at the root, cut 4-5 wedges. Peel each wedge and cut into evenly sized cubes.
2. Place in a pot of cold water with a pinch of salt and bring to the boil.
3. Cook until they are soft when pierced with a fork - this usually takes about 10-15 minutes.
4. Drain all the water, then mash with a potato masher or ricer.
5. Add the salt, pepper, cream and butter, then mix really well. Taste and adjust seasoning then serve.

# Recipe notes

# Recipe notes

SAUCES
/ DIPS

# HUMMUS

One of the fantastic things about hummus is that it is so healthy and so easy to make. This is the basic recipe so just add the alternative ingredients to make different variations. I've included some of my favourites here but you can experiment with flavours and ingredients that you like.

**Prep time 10 mins •**
**Serves 6-8**

## INGREDIENTS

- 1 x 400g can chickpeas, drain the water but keep 3 tbsp aside to add to the hummus
- 1½ tsp tahini
- 2 garlic cloves
- 3 tbsp olive oil
- Juice of ½ a lime
- 1 tsp cumin
- 6 tbsp water from the chickpea can

## METHOD

Add all the ingredients to a food processor and blend until smooth.

## Roasted Red Pepper

- 2 roasted red peppers, skinned
- ½ tsp smoked paprika or regular paprika

## Chilli & Ginger

- ½ red chilli
- ½ inch piece of root ginger
- Juice of ½ a lime

## Tomato & Basil

- 8 cherry tomatoes
- 12 fresh basil leaves

# ROASTED RED PEPPER & CHILLI RELISH

This is such a tasty and versatile relish. It goes really well with cheese - especially a nice brie or blue. Mix it through pasta to make a quick and tasty dinner or spread it on toast for a snack.

**Prep time 25 mins** •
**Cook time 45 mins** •
**Makes 2 jam jars**

## INGREDIENTS

- 6 red peppers
- 1 medium onion, chopped
- 2 garlic cloves, chopped
- 2 tbsp dark brown muscovado sugar
- 3 tbsp honey
- 2 tbsp olive oil
- ¼ red or green chilli
- 1 inch fresh ginger, grated
- 1 tsp coriander seeds
- 1.5 tsp cumin seeds or 1 tsp ground cumin

## METHOD

**1.** Roast 5 peppers and set one aside for later.
**2.** Remove the stalk and seeds from the pepper you set aside and blend it with the roast peppers and all the remaining ingredients.
**3.** Add to a non-stick or heavy bottomed pan and simmer for 45 minutes.
**4.** Allow to cool then store for up to 3 weeks in sterilised jars.

# NAPOLETANA SAUCE

## Basic

This recipe is really quick and easy to put together. If you like a chunky sauce, use a tin of chopped tomatoes or 400g of fresh tomatoes. For a smooth sauce, use tomato passata.

**Prep time 10 mins • Cook time 35 mins • Serves 4-6**

### INGREDIENTS

- 1 x 400g tin chopped tomatoes or 400g fresh tomatoes or 500g tomato passata
- 3 garlic cloves, chopped
- 2 tbsp olive oil
- 10 fresh basil leaves, chopped
- 1 tsp sugar
- Salt and freshly ground black pepper

### METHOD

**1.** Heat the oil in a pot then add the garlic. Cook for about 1 minute, without colouring the garlic.
**2.** Add the tomatoes, sugar, basil leaves, salt and pepper. Simmer for about half an hour.
■ *Serve with your favorite pasta.*

## Advanced

This sauce is bursting with flavour and can be added to fried mince to make a bolognese or to vegetables to make a veggie pasta. It is also great for a lasagne. Or simply add it to any cooked pasta for a quick and easy dinner.

**Prep time 10 mins • Cook time 1 hour 15 mins • Serves 6-8**

### INGREDIENTS

- 1 onion, chopped
- 1 x 400g tin chopped tomatoes
- 500g tomato passata
- 2 tbsp tomato purée
- 2 tsp sugar
- 20 fresh basil leaves
- 1 tsp freshly ground black pepper
- ½ tsp salt
- 1 tsp dried oregano
- 6 garlic cloves, chopped

### METHOD

**1.** Heat the oil in a pot on a medium heat then add the onion and garlic.
**2.** Gently cook without colouring for about 2-3 minutes, then add the chopped tomatoes, passata and tomato purée. Stir well and simmer for 10 minutes.
**3.** Add the sugar, salt and pepper, oregano and basil and simmer for 1 hour on a very low heat.
**4.** Blend if you like a smooth sauce or leave it as it is if you prefer it chunky.

# HOLLANDAISE SAUCE AND VARIATIONS

This easy to make, luxurious sauce is fantastic with eggs benedict or to bring vegetables like broccoli to a whole new level.

**Prep time 5 mins ● Cook time 5 mins ● Serves 4**

## INGREDIENTS
- 115g real butter
- 2 egg yolks
- 1 tsp white wine vinegar
- 1 shallot, chopped very finely (optional)

## METHOD
**1.** Melt the butter in the microwave or in a small pot.
**2.** Separate the eggs and put the yolk in a Pyrex or stainless steel bowl. Add the white wine vinegar and whisk really well.
**3.** Put some water in the bottom of a saucepan and place on the heat. Sit the bowl containing the egg yolks and vinegar on top of it so the water below is heating the bowl.
**4.** Turn off the heat under the pot and gently whisk the melted butter into the egg yolks a tiny bit at a time. Keep whisking until all the butter (not the white stuff on the bottom) has been used. You should be left with a thick butter sauce. If it starts to split at any stage, add 1tsp of boiling water.

## *Variations*

### ■ WHITE CHEDDAR HOLLANDAISE
Add 50g grated white cheddar just before you finish the sauce.

■ *This is great with quiche or an omelette.*

### ■ BACON HOLLANDAISE
Cook 2 smoked or maple rashers until really crispy then blend in a food processor and add to the sauce at the end.

■ *This is fantastic with sautéed spinach, spread on hot buttered brown soda bread. Simply drizzle the sauce over the top for a terrific snack.*

### ■ ROASTED YELLOW PEPPER AND CHILLI HOLLANDAISE
**1.** Roast 1 yellow pepper, then remove the seeds, stalk and skin.
**2.** Blend in a food processor then add ¼-½ tsp of chopped fresh chilli and add to the sauce at the end.

■ *This goes really well with halloumi or a chicken breast roasted over a bed of onions, peppers and cherry tomatoes.*

### ■ BASIL HOLLANDAISE
**1.** Add 5-10 fresh basil leaves when you add the vinegar.

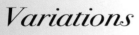

### *Liam's tip*
*Add 2 tsp of olive oil to a pan and when hot, add 20 halved cherry tomatoes, 1 chopped garlic clove and ½ a red onion, sliced. Fry for 1 minute then serve over a toasted baguette, top with basil hollandaise.*

### ■ BÉARNAISE SAUCE
You can turn a basic hollandaise sauce into béarnaise sauce by simply adding ½ tsp dried tarragon or 10 chopped fresh tarragon leaves when you aare adding the vinegar. Follow the rest of the basic recipe.

■ *This goes amazingly well with steak.*

# BLACK OLIVE TAPENADE

Olives are an acquired taste. I hated them at first but for some reason kept going back for more until eventually I discovered I loved them. I love a platter of pitta bread with homemade hummus, black olive tapenade and some cured meats. Traditional tapenade contains capers and anchovies. I have left both out as most people will struggle to find them. If you can get them then add 4 anchovy fillets and 6 capers before blending.

## INGREDIENTS
- 200g black olives, stones removed
- 5 tbsp olive oil
- 1 garlic clove
- 10g fresh thyme leaves
- 3 tbsp lemon juice
- 15g fresh parmesan cheese
- If using the capers and anchovies as per the traditional tapenade recipe, you can leave out the parmesan.

## METHOD
**1.** Put all the ingredients in a food processor or blender and blend to a rough paste.
**2.** Place in a sterilised jar and store in the fridge for up to 1 month.

# AIOLI SAUCE

Aioli sounds complicated but it's actually really simple - it's just mayonnaise with added garlic. Here, I'm going to show you how to make your own aioli from scratch and a simpler one using a jar of mayo if you don't want to go to the trouble of making your own. Serve with chunky chips, on top of a burger or add more water to thin it down and make a great salad dressing.

**Prep time 10 mins ● Serves 2-4**

## ■ HOMEMADE AIOLI

### INGREDIENTS
- 3 free range eggs
- 200ml olive oil
- 250ml sunflower oil (use all olive oil if you prefer)
- 1 tsp Dijon mustard
- 4 tbsp lemon juice
- Pinch of salt
- 3 garlic cloves
- Small bunch of parsley, chopped

### METHOD
1. Add all the ingredients except for the olive oil and sunflower oil to a food processor and blend.
2. While blending, mix the two oils together in a jug and slowly drizzle into the rest of the ingredients to form a smooth mayonnaise.

## ■ SIMPLE AIOLI MADE FROM SHOP-BOUGHT MAYONNAISE

### INGREDIENTS
- 8 tbsp mayonnaise
- 2 garlic cloves, finely chopped
- Small bunch of parsley, finely chopped

### METHOD
1. Mix all the ingredients together.
2. Add a drop of water if it is too thick.

# TOMATO RELISH

Supermarkets often have tomatoes on offer. It's the perfect time to pick some up and make this terrific tomato relish. It keeps for up to a month in the fridge and is great through pasta, spread on toast or with a cheese board.

**Prep time 10 mins ● Cook time 1 Hour ●
Makes 2 small jam jars**

### INGREDIENTS
- 12-16 large tomatoes, quartered
- 2 red onions, finely chopped
- 2 garlic cloves, finely chopped
- 4 tbsp brown sugar
- 2 tbsp red wine vinegar or cider vinegar
- 1 tbsp honey
- 1 tsp curry powder
- 1 tsp cayenne pepper
- ½ tsp mustard seeds (optional)

*Liam's tip*
*It's a good idea to label your jars with the contents, the date you made it and the expiry date.*

### METHOD
1. Place the tomatoes in a heavy-bottomed pot and add all the other ingredients, simmer for 1 hour, stirring really well every 15 minutes.
2. Remove from the heat and allow to cool before putting into sterilised jars, sealing and storing in the fridge.

# PEPPER SAUCE

This is perfect with a big juicy steak, a burger, chicken fillet or a big fat Portobello mushroom roasted in olive oil and garlic. I love pepper sauce - it's easily my favourite. It's fairly easy to make at home, too.

**Prep time 10 mins • Cook time 10 mins • Serves 4-6**

## INGREDIENTS

- 4 tsp cracked black pepper
- ½ onion, finely chopped
- 2 garlic cloves, finely chopped
- 1 tbsp olive oil
- 100ml red wine
- 250ml beef stock or 250ml of water with ½ a beef stock cube
- 250ml cream

## METHOD

**1.** Heat the oil in a pan then add the cracked black pepper, garlic and onion. Cook for 60 seconds until you really start to really smell the pepper.
**2.** Add red wine and reduce by half.
**3.** Add 250ml of beef stock or dissolve ½ a beef stock cube in 250ml of boiling water and reduce by half again.
**4.** Add the cream and reduce until thickened.
**5.** Taste and adjust seasoning, if necessary.

## ■ MUSHROOM AND SWEET PEPPER SAUCE

This sauce is perfect with most meats and is one of my signature sauces. I've simplified it here so it's perfect for serving with pork or chicken dinners.

## INGREDIENTS

- 150g button mushrooms, diced
- 3 spring onions, finely chopped
- 1 red pepper, diced
- 1 garlic clove, finely chopped
- 200ml cream
- ¼ vegetable or chicken stock cube
- Pinch of freshly ground black
- 1 tbsp olive oil

## METHOD

**1.** Heat the oil in a pan or pot then add the mushrooms, pepper, garlic and spring onion. Cook for about 2 minutes.
**2.** Add the cream and ¼ stock cube, then reduce until the sauce thickens.
**3.** Taste and adjust the seasoning if necessary.

## ■ MUSHROOM SAUCE

This sauce is really tasty with any meat and vegetable dinner.

## INGREDIENTS

- 100g button mushrooms or a 50/50 mix of wild and button, sliced
- 1 small onion or shallot, finely chopped
- 2 garlic cloves, finely chopped
- 150ml beef or vegetable stock or 150ml water with ¼ a beef or vegetable stock cube
- Pinch of freshly ground black pepper
- 2 tsp Dijon mustard
- 200ml cream
- 10 chopped chives (optional)
- 2 tbsp olive oil

## METHOD

**1.** Heat the oil in a pan or pot, then add the onions and garlic.
**2.** Cook without colouring for 2 minutes, then add the mushrooms. Cook for 3 minutes more.
**3.** Add the stock or water and reduce by half.
**4.** Add the cream and Dijon mustard and reduce until thickened
**5.** Add the chopped chives if using.
**5.** Taste and adjust the seasoning if necessary.

# HAM GLAZE

You can't beat a glazed ham, especially at Christmas time. This is a beautiful recipe and can be costly to make, but it's worth it for special occasions.

**Prep time 10 mins ● Cook time 2 mins ● Glazes 1 large ham**

## INGREDIENTS
- 6 tbsp maple syrup
- 1 tsp English mustard
- 1 tsp Dijon mustard
- 2 tbsp muscovado sugar
- ½ tsp ground clove

## METHOD
**1.** Place all the ingredients into a saucepan and heat very gently for about 2 minutes. It's ready when the sugar dissolves.
**2.** You can use it straight away or store it in the fridge in a sterilised jar for up to 2 months.

### How to glaze a ham
**1.** Boil the ham. The cooking time will depend on the weight.
**2.** Pre-heat the oven to 180°C.
**3.** When the ham is cooked place it in a roasting tin lined with grease-proof paper (this saves a horrible cleaning job later).
**4.** Score the fat with a knife and use a pastry brush to coat the entire ham in the glaze.
**5.** Bake in the oven for 15 minutes then remove from the oven and brush with some more glaze.
**6.** Return to the oven cook for a further 15 minutes, or longer, depending on the size of the ham. It should be nice and crispy when ready.

## Liam's tip
*Ham is one of my favourite meats. I never buy the packets of processed, sliced ham. Instead, I watch out for when proper ham is on special offer at the butcher or supermarket and I buy a couple of them. I cook it, allow to cool and slice it all thinly. It freezes really well so I portion it into bags and pop into my freezer. I just defrost in the fridge and use when I need it. It's delicious in sandwiches, in a pasta dish or in a chicken and ham pie.*

# ■ BÉCHAMEL SAUCE

Béchamel, or white sauce, is the base for so many other sauces. It's milk-based and used in everything from a lasagne, to garlic potatoes and cauliflower cheese. It's a really easy sauce to master and it's very quick to make. The classic way to make it is by using a clove studded onion to infuse flavour, although I haven't seen this done since college 20-odd years ago. You can use a vegetable or chicken stock cube at home to make it easier.

## INGREDIENTS
- **500ml milk**
- **30g butter**
- **30g flour**
- **1 vegetable or chicken stock cube**
- **Pinch of nutmeg (optional)**
- **1 onion studded with 8 cloves (optional)**

## METHOD
**1.** Place the milk and stock cube in a heavy-bottomed pot and place on the heat to simmer.
**2.** If using the studded onion, stick the pointy end of the cloves into the onion, then place it in the milk.
**3.** Slowly melt the butter in another pot, taking care not to brown or burn it.
**4.** Add the flour to the butter and stir for about 1 minute. You will end up with a yellow paste or roux.
**5.** When the milk is close to boiling, remove the onion then pour the milk into the pot with the roux whisking briskly while you do so. You should end up with a smooth sauce that should coat the back of a spoon.
**6.** If it is too thick, add a little more milk. If it is lumpy, blend with a stick blender or pass the sauce through a sieve.

## *Variations*

### ■ PARSLEY SAUCE
Follow the béchamel recipe then add a good bunch of finely chopped parsley at the last stage after you blend the sauce or pass it thought the sieve. Allow to simmer for 10–15 minutes.

### ■ MUSTARD SAUCE
You can use English or grain mustard to make this. Simply add 1 tbsp of grain mustard or 2 tsp of English. Whisk whichever you use into the sauce at the end and leave to simmer for 10–15 minutes.
■ *This is great with bacon and cabbage or pork chops, or over peppers and mushrooms before baking them.*

### ■ CHEESE SAUCE
Add 100-150g of grated cheddar cheese. I always use white for a more natural looking sauce though you can use red cheddar if it's all you have in the fridge.
■ *This is brilliant over broccoli, or used in a cauliflower cheese. It is also ideal for a macaroni cheese.*

### ■ BLUE CHEESE SAUCE
This is one of my favourite sauces. Simply add 75-150g of a good blue cheese to the béchamel when finished. Simmer for 10 minutes then serve.
■ *This is fantastic with a steak, chicken, prawns, or grilled whole portobello mushrooms.*

### ■ SUPREME SAUCE
Slice 100g of button mushrooms and finely chop ½ an onion. Cook, without colouring, in a hot pan with 1 tbsp of olive oil. After the onions turn translucent, add the sauce and stir well. Simmer for 10–15 minutes.
■ *This goes really well with a chicken or a pasta bake.*

### ■ VELOUTÉ
Velouté is almost the exact same as béchamel, only it is made with stock instead of milk. It's often used in classic

and many complicated dishes. I prefer to look at it as a way to make sauces more interesting.

If I'm making a parsley sauce for bacon and cabbage, I sometimes use half milk and half bacon water to give it extra flavour.

Another way of looking at velouté is as a lower fat option to a béchamel. If you choose to do this then I would recommend adding a drop of cream to give it a little more life.

To make a velouté sauce, follow the exact same method for the béchamel, but replace the milk with fresh stock or dissolve a stock cube in 500ml water and use instead of the milk. You can make any of the sauces mentioned above using a velouté.

## ■ MUSTARD SAUCE FOR BACON AND CABBAGE

Place your bacon on to boil. After about half an hour strain the water it's been cooking in into another pot then top the bacon up with fresh water and stick back on to boil again. Measure out 250ml of the water you strained from the bacon and mix with 250ml of fresh milk. Follow the recipe for béchamel sauce but use this mix instead of milk. Add 1 tbsp of English mustard at the end, simmer for 10 minutes.

# GARLIC BUTTER

Buying pre-made garlic butter is so much more expensive than doing it yourself at home. It's so quick and easy as well. It's great with a steak, chicken, pasta and bread

**Prep time 5 mins •
Makes 500g
or 1lb Garlic Butter**

## INGREDIENTS
- 1lb butter, softened but not melted
- 8–10 garlic cloves
- Handful of fresh parsley, stalks removed

## METHOD
**1.** Pop the garlic and parsley into a food processor and blitz until almost smooth.
**2.** Cut the butter into 8 pieces and pop each piece in the processor one at a time, until the whole lot is blended.
**3.** At this point you can stick it in a tub and scoop it out as needed, but if you want to do it the way I do it and how it's done in restaurants, read the following steps.
**4.** Lay out a long sheet of greaseproof paper onto your counter, roughly measuring from your finger tips to your elbow.
**5.** Using a spatula, remove the butter from the food processor and lay in in a 6 inch line, centred but towards one edge of the paper.
**6.** Roll the paper, starting at the same side the butter is on until it's completely rolled.
**7.** Grab either end and twist each in opposite directions. This will start to compress the garlic butter. It's up to you how thick you want it. When done, pop it in the fridge to set.

**8.** It will keep as long as the date on the butter packet. When needed, simply cut slices off. They look great when presented on vegetables or a steak.

## ■ CORIANDER, LIME AND CHILLI BUTTER
This is great with fish, chicken, veggies or even spread on crusty bread before toasting it under the grill.

### INGREDIENTS
- 1lb real butter
- ½ red chilli (use the whole thing if you like it hot)
- ½ inch ginger or galangal
- 2 garlic cloves
- Good bunch of coriander
- 1 lime, zest and juice
- 1 tbsp fish sauce

## METHOD
**1.** Blitz everything except the butter in the food processor then follow method 2 for the garlic butter above. (Remember to only use the zest and juice of the lime)
**2.** You can roll this or stick it in a tub.

## ■ GARLIC SPREAD

### INGREDIENTS
- 1 tub of supermarket spread, roughly 500g
- 8–10 garlic cloves
- Small bunch of parsley, stalks removed

### METHOD
Follow the same method aas the garlic butter, only don't roll it as it doesn't set very well. Just stick it back into the tub the spread came in.

## ◼ BRANDY BUTTER

Chirstmas wouldn't be Christmas without proper brandy butter. Serve it on top of the pudding or with mince pies, or a nice slice of Christmas cake. You can even pop a dollop of it into your coffee.

### INGREDIENTS
- 150g real butter
- 150g Icing sugar
- 4 tbsp brandy
- 2 tsp really hot or boiling water

### METHOD
Cream the butter and icing sugar together with a hand blender, whisk or stand mixer. Add the brandy and water, then mix until smooth.
◼ *I like to wrap it, but you can also pop it into a container and scoop it out when needed*.

## ◼ LEMON BUTTER

Ideal with chicken or fish, or spread on a chicken salad sandwich.

### INGREDIENTS
- 150g real butter, softened but not melted
- Zest of 1 lemon and juice of half
- Small bunch of parsley

### METHOD
Chop the zest and parsley as fine as you can then mix with the butter and the lemon juice. You can also use a food processor.
Store in a tub in the fridge until needed.

# ONION MARMALADE

This is the perfect accompaniment to most cheese, especially a good blue. I never serve a cheese board without it. It takes hours to cook out, so I strongly suggest you make it in bulk as it will keep in a jar in the fridge for two months once left unopened. You will get 10 jam jars from this recipe-halve the recipe if that is too much for you. The ingredients are cheap so why not make the full batch and give to friends and family or give it as a special gift.

**Prep time 30 mins ● Cook time 4 hours ● Makes 8-10 jars**

### INGREDIENTS
- 2kg onions (I use white but use red if you prefer)
- 75ml olive oil
- 150g brown sugar
- 8 tbsp honey
- 3 star anise
- 3 bay leaves
- 2 tsp cayenne pepper
- 200ml white wine vinegar
- 100ml white wine or port
- 75ml balsamic vinegar

### METHOD
1. Peel all the onions and discard the skins. Cut each onion in half then slice from the side ensuring you cut them thinly.
2. Heat the olive oil in the pot to a medium heat then add the onions and give them a good stir to coat them in oil. Cover with the lid and leave on a low heat for 10 minutes. Stir well then leave for another 10 minutes.
3. Add the sugar, star anise, bay leaves and the cayenne pepper. Stir, cover and leave for 20 minutes, stirring halfway through.
4. Pour the white wine vinegar, balsamic and white wine or port into the pot, stir again then cover and leave on a very low heat for 2 hours. Stir every half hour or more if the marmalade is sticking to the bottom.
5. After 2 hours add the honey, stir and taste. This is the time to add more of anything you feel it may need. Add more vinegar or sugar as desired, just remember the flavours change slightly when served cool.
6. Put back on the heat, uncovered and leave for 1 hour more, stirring every half hour again.
7. Taste and adjust flavour one last time then let the marmalade cool before portioning into jars. Store in a fridge for up to 2 months. I like to store it for up to 2 weeks before using as this helps the flavours intensify even more.

*Liam's tip*

*Slice and fry some mushrooms in garlic and a little chilli, then serve on toast with a dollop of these onions for a nice snack.*

■ Cooking well on a budget is all about striking the right balance between quality ingredients and buying own-brand products in supermarkets. It's about mixing and matching and being smart with flavours. Oil is one of those things I don't compromise on because I believe there's not much point in choosing things like fish and meat wisely and then ruining the taste by frying it in something of poor quality. I love rapeseed oil and I've tried out loads of different brands but this is my new favourite.

Derrycamma Farm is located near Castlebellingham in Co. Louth. It's owned and managed by Patrick and Carol Rooney and although it's not an organic farm, they use a lot of organic practices and use natural and green fertilisers, which is fantastic.

I used rapeseed oil in many of the recipes in this book. Whether it's for a salad dressing, or frying meat and fish, I love the flavours and Derrycamma Farm oil is delicious. It even comes in different infused flavours, which are seriously delicious. Derrycamma Farm has won awards for a reason. Rapeseed oil is suitable for cooking at really high temperatures too, which is great. And as you may know, I have heart troubles and rapeseed oil has loads of Omega 3s and is lower in saturated fat than most other popular cooking oils. That's a huge plus for me.

# DERRYCAMMA FARM
## CASTLEBELLINGHAM, CO. LOUTH

Phone 087 822 3875 www.rapeseed-oil.ie

# Recipe notes

# Recipe notes

# Recipe notes

DESSERT

# MAPLE AND CHOCOLATE TART WITH CARAMELISED HAZELNUTS

**Prep time 1 hour 30 mins
• Cook time 30 mins •
Setting time 1 hour •
Serves 8-10**

## INGREDIENTS
The filling
- **750g milk chocolate**
- **250ml cream**
- **2 tbsp maple syrup**
- **50g hazelnuts**
The pastry
- **250g plain flour**
- **125g butter, cut into cubes**
- **1 egg**
- **Pinch of salt**
- **1 tsp sugar**
The topping
- **200g hazelnuts**
- **2 tsp dark brown muscovado sugar**
- **2 tsp light brown or white sugar**
- **2 tbsp maple syrup**
- **Icing suger to dust**

## METHOD
### The pastry
**1.** Pre-heat your oven to 180°C or gas mark 4.
**2.** Sieve the flour and salt into a bowl, then add the butter.
**3.** Using the tips of your fingers, rub the butter into the flour until it is grainy and free of large butter lumps.
**4.** Add the egg, mix using a metal utensil to keep the pastry as cool as possible. It should form a smooth dough that's not too dry or not too wet. Add a drop of cold water if needed. Wrap in cling film and leave to rest in the fridge for at least half an hour.
**6.** Remove the pastry from the fridge and roll it out to fit a 23cm fluted tin (those are the ones with crinkles around the edges).

**7.** The pastry should hang slightly over the edges of the tin. Gently prick the base of the pastry with a fork about six times.
**8.** Cover the pastry in baking parchment and then fill the baking parchment with either baking beads, if you have them, or uncooked rice, ensuring you fill it right to the edges. This stops the pastry from rising and is known as blind baking.
**9.** Trim the edges of the pastry and blind bake in the oven for 15 minutes.
**10.** Remove the baking parchment slowly as it may stick, then return the pastry base to the oven for 10 more minutes or until the centre has dried out.
**11.** Allow to cool on a wire rack.

### The filling
**1.** Heat around ½ a pint of water in

a small pot. Place a stainless steel or heavy plastic bowl on top, ensuring no water gets into the bowl.

**2.** Break the chocolate up into squares and place into the bowl to melt.

**3.** Meanwhile, chop 50g of the hazelnuts in a food processor and put them into another saucepan with the cream and maple syrup. Bring to the boil gently, then remove from the heat.

**4.** Remove the bowl with the melted chocolate from the heat and add the cream and hazelnut mix. Whisk until smooth.

**5.** Pour this mixture into the cooked pastry base, then allow to set in the fridge for about 1 hour.

### The topping

**1.** Place the hazelnuts on a frying pan, add the sugars and maple syrup. Heat until the sugar dissolves usually about 1 minute - taking care not to burn the sugar.

**2.** Allow to cool a little then place the hazelnuts on top of the tart so they evenly cover the top.

■ *Dust with icing suger and serve with whipped cream.*

# APPLE CRUMBLE

Prep time 1 hour 20 mins •
Cook time 45 mins • Serves 10-12

## INGREDIENTS

**The pastry**
- 200g flour
- 100g butter or margarine
- 1 egg

**The filling**
- 5-6 cooking apples
- 100g light brown sugar
- 3 tbsp honey
- 50g raisins
- 50ml cold water
- 3 tbsp cornflour + 1 tbsp cold water

**The topping**
- 150g plain flour
- 100g muscovado sugar
- 75g butter

## METHOD

### The pastry

1. Pre-heat your oven to 180°C or gas mark 4.

2. Sieve the flour and salt into a bowl then cut the butter into smaller pieces and add to the same bowl.

3. Using the tips of your fingers rub the butter into the flour until it is grainy and free of large butter lumps.

4. Add the egg, mix using a metal utensil to keep the pastry as cool as possible. It should form a smooth dough that's not too dry or not too wet. Add a drop of cold water if needed. Wrap in cling film and leave to rest in the fridge for at least one hour.

6. Remove the pastry from the fridge and roll it out to fit a 23cm fluted tin (those are the ones with crinkles around the edges). The pastry should hang slightly over the edges of the tin. Gently prick the base of the pastry with a fork about six times.

7. Cover the pastry in baking parchment and then fill the baking parchment with either baking beads, if you have them, or un-cooked rice, ensuring you fill it right to the edges. This stops the pastry from rising and is known as blind baking.

8. Trim the edges of the pastry and blind bake in your oven for 15 minutes.

9. Remove the baking parchment slowly as it may stick, then return the pastry base to the oven for 10 more minutes or until the centre has dried out.

10. Allow to cool on a wire rack

### The filling

1. Peel and core the apples, then cut into small squares. Add these to a pot with the all of the filling in-gredients, apart from the cornflour and the 1 tbsp of water. Cook on a medium heat for 10 minutes.

2. Add 1 tbsp of water to the corn-flour and form a paste, then add this to the apples and mix really well.

3. Set aside to cool a little while you make the topping.

### The topping

1. Add the flour, sugar and butter to a bowl and, using the tips of your fingers, mix until you are left with a small crumb.

### Putting it all together

1. Pour the apple mix into the base then, starting in the centre, add the crumble mix, and work your way outwards until you've used it all.

2. Spread it out to the edges so that you have evenly covered the entire pie.

3. Bake for 20–25 minutes.

■ **Serve hot with fresh cream or ice-cream.**

# PECAN PAVLOVA

The difference between meringue and pavlova is that pavlova has a soft and squishy centre. This is achieved by adding cornflour, which gives it a wonderful marshmallow type effect. I'm not a fan of meringues but love a proper pavlova - that gooey centre gets me every time. The addition of pecan nuts in this recipe brings it to a whole new level. I can almost guarantee that this won't last long after you make it.

**Prep time 15 mins • Cook time 1 hour 30 mins • Serves 12**

## INGREDIENTS
- 8 egg whites
- 450g caster sugar
- 2 tsp vanilla extract
- 2 tsp cornflour
- 2 tsp white vinegar
- 100g pecan nuts, ground in a blender or food processor
- 500ml fresh cream, whipped
- A mixture of fresh fruit

## METHOD
1. Pre-heat your oven to 110ºC gas mark 1.
2. Place the egg whites into a very clean and dry bowl and whisk until stiff peaks form, about 3-4 minutes.
3. While still whisking the eggs, add the caster sugar a little at a time until the mix is stiff and glossy - this takes about 6 minutes.
4. Sieve the cornflour into the mix, then add the vinegar and vanilla extract. Whisk for about 1 more minute.

# CHOCOLATE CUSTARD

Homemade custard is so much better than the packaged variety. It's so delicious and so versatile. Make it with white chocolate and serve it in a glass with fresh strawberries and cream on top, or make a dark chocolate version and use it to make trifle with a twist. It goes great on its own with crushed up Oreos.

**Prep time 5 mins •
Cook time 10 mins • Serves 4**

## INGREDIENTS

- 4 eggs
- 75g caster sugar
- 250ml milk
- 2 tsp vanilla extract or
  ½ vanilla pod
- 75g milk, white or dark chocolate
- 150g butter

## METHOD

**1.** Heat the cream in a pot with the vanilla.
**2.** Meanwhile, in a separate bowl and using a hand-mixer, whisk the eggs and sugar together until they are smooth.
**3.** When the cream is close to boiling, pour a ladle of it into the bowl with the eggs and sugar and mix well.
**4.** Pour this into the pot with the cream and whisk really well. While heating, add the chocolate and whisk until smooth.
**5.** The custard is ready when it starts to coat the back of a spoon. At this point whisk in the butter. I like mine a little thicker so I cook it a little longer to get it to the right consistency, then remove it from the heat immediately. Don't overcook it or you will end up with scrambled eggs.

**5.** Using a spatula, fold in the ground pecan nuts. Be really careful not to remove all the air as it will collapse.
**6.** Line a baking tray with baking parchment. Using a teaspoon, dot a tiny bit of the mixture onto the tray so that the baking parchment sticks to it. You don't want it to blow onto your pavlova when baking.
**7.** Spread the mixture into 2 even shapes onto the trays. I like to make circles but you can do it in any shape you want. (You can even make individual portions if you prefer but reduce the cooking time to 45 minutes for a small bowl-sized shape.)
**8.** Bake for about 1 hour 30 minutes, turning halfway through so it cooks evenly.
**9.** When the time is up, turn off the oven but leave the pavlova in and allow it to cool in the oven. This will stop it from cracking as it cools.
**10.** When cooled, remove from the oven and gently remove the parchment.
**11** Spread whipped cream on one then add your choice of fruit, before placing the other piece on top.

■ *Decorate this with fresh cream and fruit then serve.*

# POACHED PEARS, RASPBERRY AND MINT COULIS WITH HONEY GREEK YOGHURT

This was the crew's favourite dessert during the photoshoot. The photographer ate a few of them. The best bit is that these are a lot healthier than most desserts and they taste simply fantastic. If you're looking to impress someone, this is an ideal dessert as it looks like something you'd get served in a lovely restaurant.

**Prep time 20 mins • Cook time 30 mins • Serves 6**

## INGREDIENTS
- **6 pears**
- **100ml white wine**
- **1 vanilla pod or 2 tsp vanilla extract**
- **100g sugar**
- **100g frozen or 200g fresh raspberries**
- **15 mint leaves**
- **150g Greek yoghurt**
- **3 tbsp honey for the sauce**
- **3 tbsp honey for the yoghurt**

## METHOD
**1.** Add the wine, sugar, vanilla and water to a medium pot and place on a low heat.
**2.** Peel the pears, ensuring you keep the stalk attached as shown in the picture, then place in the liquid. Add more water if you need to, to ensure they are covered.
**3.** Bring to the boil, cover and simmer for 20–30 minutes.
**4.** Meanwhile, if using frozen berries, place them in a pot of boiling water and put back on the heat for 2 minutes. Drain, then place in a food processor, add the honey and mint then blend until smooth. Taste and if they're too bitter, add more honey until you are happy with the flavour. Set aside for later.
**5.** Set aside for later.
**6.** Mix the yoghurt and the rest of the honey together and set aside then gently remove the pears from the liquid and set to one side, too.
**7.** Turn the heat back up and boil until the cooking liquid is reduced by about half.
**8.** To assemble the dish, place a dollop of yoghurt in the centre of the bowl, then an outer layer of the raspberry coulis. Place the pear on top of the yoghurt, then add some little dots of yoghurt around the coulis, as shown in the picture.
**9.** Just before you serve, pour a little of the cooking liquid over the pear. Serve the remaining cooking liquid in a bowl on the side and garnish with a fresh mint leaf.

# APPLE SPONGE

I don't have a huge sweet tooth but I do love apple sponge. I make mine a little differently than most as I use the sponge as a topping to what is basically an apple pie base. I think it makes it so much better. It adds layers of texture and flavour that you don't expect from a simple apple sponge.

**Prep time 20 mins • Cook time 1 hour 20 mins • Serves 8-10**

## INGREDIENTS

### The base
- 150g plain flour
- 75g butter or margarine
- 1 egg
- 1 tsp sugar
- Pinch of salt

### The filling
- 6 large cooking apples
- 115g sugar
- 1 tsp cinnamon
- 2 tsp vanilla extract
- 25g butter

### The sponge
- 150g self raising flour
- 150g butter
- 150g caster sugar
- 3 large eggs
- Pinch of salt

## METHOD

**1.** Start with the base as it needs time to chill once made. Place the flour, salt and sugar in a bowl and rub in the butter with the tips of your fingers until you are left with coarse flour or sandy texture.

**2.** Add the egg and knead it to form a dough. Wrap it in cling film and place in the fridge for 1 hour.

**3.** Pre-heat your oven to 180°C or gas mark 4.

**4.** When the dough is chilled, roll it out to fit a 23cm fluted tart tin, flan tin or quiche dish.

**5.** Blind bake this by pricking the pastry with a fork a few times and covering it with baking parchment. Then fill this with baking beads or raw rice and pop it in the oven for 15 minutes. While it's cooking, start working on the filling.

### The filling

**1.** Peel and core the apples then cut into a small dice.

**2.** Place the cut apples in a medium pot with the vanilla extract and sugar then add 4 tbsp of water. Cook on a medium heat for 10 minutes.

**3.** Add the cinnamon and butter then mix well until the butter dissolves, then set it aside.

### The sponge

**1.** Using a hand mixer or a stand mixer, cream the sugar and butter until it turns pale and fluffy.

**2.** Turn the speed on low then add 1 egg at a time until all 3 have been added. If the mixture is too thick and heavy, add 3 tsp of cold water.

**3.** Sieve the flour and salt then slowly and gently fold them into the mixture.

### Putting it all together

**1.** Pour the apple mix on top of the pastry base.

**2.** Top this with sponge and bake for about 50 minutes, depending on your oven. If using gas make sure you turn the sponge every 15 minutes so it cooks evenly.

■ **Serve with vanilla ice cream or home-made custard (See page 235).**

### Liam's tip
*You can tell it's cooked when you stuck a knife into the centre of the sponge and it comes out clean.*

# Recipe notes

# Recipe notes

*Tandoori chicken page 90*

*Slow cooker bbq ribs page 80*

*Hazelnut tart  page 230*

*Cajun chicken burger page 94*

*Healthy chicken and pasta bake page 98*

*Vegetarian frittata page 48*

*Bruschetta page 42*

Pecan pavlova page 234

*Thai green curry page 103*

*Turkey noodles page 140*

*Lamb samosas page 57*

*Poached pears page 236*

# LIAM'S OVEN TEMPERATURES AND CONVERSIONS

A conversion chart is as essential in a kitchen as a good knife or frying pan.

## Dimensions

| Imperial | Metric |
|----------|--------|
| ⅛ inch | 3 mm |
| ¼ inch | 5 mm |
| ½ inch | 1 cm |
| ¾ inch | 2 cm |
| 1 inch | 2.5 cm |
| 1¼ inch | 3 cm |
| 1½ inch | 4 cm |
| 1¾ inch | 4.5 cm |
| 2 inch | 5 cm |
| 2½ inch | 6 cm |
| 3 inch | 7.5 cm |
| 3½ inch | 9 cm |
| 4 inch | 10 cm |
| 5 inch | 13 cm |
| 6 inch | 15 cm |
| 6½ inch | 16 cm |
| 7 inch | 18 cm |
| 7½ inch | 19 cm |
| 8 inch | 20 cm |
| 9 inch | 23 cm |
| 10 inch | 25½ cm |
| 11 inch | 28 cm |
| 12 inch | 30 cm |

## Weights

| Imperial | Metric |
|----------|--------|
| 1/2 oz | 10 g |
| 3/4 oz | 20 g |
| 1 oz | 25 g |
| 1.5 oz | 40 g |
| 2 oz | 50 g |
| 2.5 oz | 60 g |
| 3 oz | 75 g |
| 4 oz | 110 g |
| 4.5 oz | 125 g |
| 5 oz | 150 g |
| 6 oz | 175 g |
| 7 oz | 200 g |
| 8 oz | 225 g |
| 9 oz | 250 g |
| 10 oz | 275 g |
| 12 oz | 350 g |
| 1 lb | 450 g |
| 1lb 8 oz | 700 g |
| 2lb | 900 g |
| 3lb | 1.35 kg |

- Oven temperatures through my book are based on a fan or gas oven.
- All measurements are level, so don't go mad and add too much by filling those measuring spoons up too much.
- If using a conventional oven, I suggest you increase the temperature by 20°C but it's best you get to know your own oven and adjust the times and temperatures accordingly.
- I use large free range eggs.
- All butter is salted unless otherwise stated
- I've used full fat milk in each recipe.
- Never mix metric or imperial measurements, stick with one or the other.
- Take your time and read each recipe in full before starting.
- PM me on Facebook or DM me on Twitter if you need my help. I answer every single message.

# Volume

| Imperial | Metric |
|---|---|
| 2 fl oz | 55 ml |
| 3 fl oz | 75 ml |
| 5 fl oz (¼ pint) | 150 ml |
| 10 fl oz (½ pint) | 275 ml |
| 1 pint | 570 ml |
| 1¼ pint | 725 ml |
| 1¾ pint | 1 litre |
| 2 pint | 1.2 litre |
| 2½ pint | 1.5 litre |
| 4 pint | 2.25 litre |

# Oven Temperatures

| Gas | °F | °C |
|---|---|---|
| 1 | 275°F | 140°C |
| 2 | 300°F | 150°C |
| 3 | 325°F | 170°C |
| 4 | 350°F | 180°C |
| 5 | 375°F | 190°C |
| 6 | 400°F | 200°C |
| 7 | 425°F | 220°C |
| 8 | 450°F | 230°C |
| 9 | 475°F | 240°C |

# ESSENTIAL STOCK CUPBOARD INGREDIENTS

■ Having a well-stocked store cupboard will have you on the right road to making delicious, home-cooked meals. If you have all the basics at home, all you have to do during your weekly shop is buy in fresh ingredients like meat, fish, fruits, vegetables and dairy.

Shopping around for great deals on things like chopped tomatoes and generic dry goods can save you a fortune on your food bills. You can then buy quality, key ingredients that I find make all the difference when you're cooking. For example, I stock up on cheap, own-brand staples from various supermarkets, but I always invest in a good oil for cooking. There's no point in having a lovely piece of meat or fish and then frying it in something of low quality that doesn't taste great. My absolute favourite is rapeseed oil and I used it for many of the recipes in the book. You can really taste the difference.

Other ingredients that I usually make sure to invest in wisely are my meat, fish and cheeses. But for basic store cupboard ingredients, I always shop around to make sure that I have what I need in the house to whip up whatever tickles my fancy - be it a Chinese dish, an Indian or a hearty Irish stew.

I always have the following in my store cupboard:

## Tinned food

Chopped tomatoes
Coconut milk
Chickpeas
Kidney beans
White butter beans
Tuna/salmon/sardines
Tomato passata
Tomato purée

## Dressings/Sauce

Red wine vinegar
White wine vinegar
Cider vinegar
Balsamic vinegar
Soy sauce
Fish sauce
Oyster sauce

## Baking

Plain flour
Self raising flour
Wholemeal flour
Cornflour
Baking Powder
Bread soda
Yeast
Raisins or sultanas
Honey
Maple syrup
Sugar - muscovado, light
brown, white, caster

## Starches

Pasta
Rice - long grain or
basmati or jasmine
Couscous
Noodles - egg or rice

## Dry Herbs

Basil
Oregano
Thyme
Parsley
Coriander

## Spices

Cayenne pepper
Paprika/Chilli
Cinnamon sticks
and ground cinnamon
Cumin
Curry powder
Garam masala
Turmeric
Nutmeg
Green cardamom
Cloves whole /ground
Garlic powder

## Recommended

Smoked paprika
Mace
Mustard seeds
Poppy seeds
Sunflower seeds
Szechuan or rose pepper

## Extras

Cracked black pepper
Whole pepper mill
Stock cubes - beef,
chicken, fish
and vegetable
Sea salt mill

# LIAM'S TOP TIPS ON HOW TO REDUCE THE COST OF YOUR WEEKLY SHOPPING BILL

■ When I was living in Dublin and surviving on what was left of my dole payment after I'd paid my bills, friends were always amazed at the spreads I could turn out on such a tight budget. My apartment was always a place where people gathered after having a few pints as I could whip up something delicious for everyone in minutes - and it didn't cost an arm and a leg. I always had a stock cupboard full of basics and a freezer stuffed with meat I'd bought in bulk when it was on special offer. So it was never too much trouble to whip up my signature burgers or a curry or some killer steak sandwiches and homemade chips.

I started posted recipes for friends on Facebook because they wanted to learn how to create these quick and easy, budget meals at home for their own families - and BiaMaith was born. I'm a professional chef and made a living out of cooking fantastic food for a profit. Taking those skills to the home kitchen has meant that I've become an expert at cooking good food frugally. Here, I'm sharing some of my top tips to help you save money on your own food bills. It's what BiaMaith is all about.

- Always make a meal plan for the week. Decide in advance what you are having and then make your shopping list accordingly. Stick to the list as best you can.

- Do your homework and find out what different supermarkets have on special offer on a given week and plan your meals around these.
- A lot of supermarkets have their own apps these days and they're so handy for checking the latest deals.

- Be wise with your meal plans. For example, if one recipe calls for half a bell pepper, choose another recipe that will use the other half so that you're not wasting food.

- Don't shop too often. A big shop is more cost effective than popping in and out a few times a week for things you need. The more you go into a shop, the more money you're likely to spend. You're also more likely to buy items you don't actually need, which can lead to more food waste.

- Shop around. Get to know supermarkets' own brands. You can get great value on things like dried pasta, tins of food etc.

- Keep a hold of vouchers for money off items. Sometimes newspapers have €10 off vouchers. Or some supermarkets offer €10 vouchers for every €50 spent. Be clever about these offers and you could save a load of money.

- Shops often discount perfectly good food when it's coming up to its use by date. You could buy good quality items and freeze them, or cook them straight away. I would advise not buying chicken and prawns like this though.

- Make sure you have a well stocked store cupboard full of versatile ingredients. This way you're able to pull out a few tins or cans out and be well on your way to cook a delicious meal. Check out my essentials guide to stocking a cupboard on page 252.

- Don't go shopping when you're hungry - you're more likely to make impulse purchases.

- It can often be difficult to figure out what the cheapest product is by simply looking at the price tags of a load of different brands. One way to check for the best value is to look at the price per kilo/price per litre, etc. This tells you the true cost of the item and saves on any confusion or doubt.

- Double up on ingredients. When meat is on special offer, fill your freezer. If mince is on special offer, for example, you could make double batches of freezer friendly foods like lasagne, bolognese sauce, burgers or chilli con carne.

- Bring your own shopping bags. Keep them in the boot of your car so that you've always got a few handy.

- And, of course, I've saved the most important tip of all for last: Like the BiaMaith Facebook page and keep a close eye on www.biamaith.ie for loads of great, budget-friendly recipes.

| | Breakfast | Lunch | Dinner Main | Dinner Side | Dinner Side | Dinner Side |
|---|---|---|---|---|---|---|
| **Monday** | Porridge and Berries | Ham and Cheese Quiche (use Sunday's left-over ham) p50 | Chicken and Pasta Bake p99 | Garlic Bread | Green salad | |
| **Tuesday** | Berry Smoothies - (see recipe on www.BiaMaith.ie) | Pasta Salad (use leftover penne from the night before) | Bangers and Mash p127 | Bacon & Cheese Mash p185 | Onion Marmalade p219 | Sautéed Cabbage with smoked bacon p192 |
| **Wednesday** | Toast with Vegetable Spread | Cold Sausage Sandwich with homemade tomato relish p213 (use unused sausages from Tuesday) | Slow Cooked BBQ Beef Ribs p82 | Baked Potato with garlic butter | Corn on the cob | |
| **Thursday** | Pancakes with honey Greek yoghurt (see recipe on BiaMaith.ie) | Roasted Vegetable and Olive Frittata p49 | Turkey Burger p142 | Side Salad with crispy croutons dipped in sweet chilli sauce | | |
| **Friday** | Toasted Soda Bread p27 and Scrambled eggs ( use unused eggs from Thursdays lunch) | Roasted Root Vegetable soup and white soda bread p32 | Seafood Lasagne p159 | Toasted crispy baguette with lemon butter, basil and fresh parmesan | Small Caesar Salad p16 | |
| **Saturday** | Kids' favorite cereal as a treat | Minestrone Soup and Garlic Bread (Use remaining veg from other dishes) p30 | Southern Fried Chicken p93 | Root Vegetable & Sweet Potato Fries (use the unused root veg) | Garlic Aioli p213 | Homemade Coleslaw |
| **Sunday** | Mushrooms Poached in Garlic and black pepper milk with white soda bread (see recipe on BiaMaith.ie) | Hummus and Crispy Bread p204 | Roast Rib of Beef p81 | Horseradish Mash p185 | Sage & Onion Stuffing (use any leftover soda bread to make the breadcrumbs) p196 | Cauliflower Cheese p194  Honey & Rosemary Roast Carrots & Parsnips p191 |

# CALENDAR OF AVAILABILITY GUIDE FOR FRUIT & VEGETABLES

## Vegetables

| | JAN | FEB | MAR | APR | MAY | JUN | JUL | AUG | SEP | OCT | NOV | DEC |
|---|---|---|---|---|---|---|---|---|---|---|---|---|
| Asparagus | | | | APR | MAY | JUN | JUL | | | | | |
| Aubergines | | | | APR | MAY | JUN | JUL | AUG | SEP | | | |
| Beetroot | JAN | FEB | MAR | APR | MAY | JUN | JUL | AUG | SEP | OCT | NOV | DEC |
| Broad Beans | | | | | MAY | JUN | JUL | AUG | SEP | | | |
| Broccoli (Green) | | | | | MAY | JUN | JUL | AUG | SEP | OCT | NOV | DEC |
| Broccoli (Purple Sprouting) | JAN | FEB | MAR | APR | | | | | | OCT | NOV | DEC |
| Brussels Sprouts | JAN | FEB | MAR | APR | | | | AUG | SEP | OCT | NOV | DEC |
| Cabbage | JAN | FEB | MAR | APR | MAY | JUN | JUL | AUG | SEP | OCT | NOV | DEC |
| Carrots | JAN | FEB | MAR | APR | | JUN | JUL | AUG | SEP | OCT | NOV | DEC |
| Cauliflower | JAN | FEB | MAR | APR | MAY | JUN | JUL | AUG | SEP | OCT | NOV | DEC |
| Celeriac | JAN | FEB | MAR | | | | | | SEP | OCT | NOV | DEC |
| French Beans | | | | | MAY | JUN | JUL | AUG | SEP | OCT | | |
| Kale | JAN | FEB | MAR | APR | | | | AUG | SEP | OCT | NOV | DEC |
| Kohl – Rabi | | | | | | JUN | JUL | AUG | SEP | OCT | NOV | |
| Leeks | JAN | FEB | MAR | APR | | | | AUG | SEP | OCT | NOV | DEC |
| Mangetout | | | | | | JUN | JUL | AUG | SEP | OCT | | |
| Marrows | | | | | | | JUL | AUG | SEP | OCT | NOV | |
| Mushrooms | JAN | FEB | MAR | APR | MAY | JUN | JUL | AUG | SEP | OCT | NOV | DEC |
| Onions | JAN | FEB | MAR | APR | MAY | | JUL | AUG | SEP | OCT | NOV | DEC |
| Pak Choi | JAN | | | APR | MAY | JUN | JUL | AUG | SEP | OCT | NOV | DEC |
| Parsnips | JAN | FEB | MAR | APR | | | JUL | AUG | SEP | OCT | NOV | DEC |
| Peas | | | | | | JUN | JUL | AUG | SEP | OCT | | |
| Potatoes (Main Crop) | JAN | FEB | MAR | APR | MAY | JUN | JUL | AUG | SEP | OCT | NOV | DEC |
| Potatoes (New Season) | | | | | MAY | JUN | JUL | AUG | | | | |
| Rhubarb | | | MAR | APR | MAY | JUN | JUL | AUG | SEP | OCT | | |
| Runner Beans | | | | | | JUN | JUL | AUG | SEP | OCT | | |
| Shallots | | | | | MAY | JUN | JUL | AUG | SEP | | | |
| Spinach | | | | APR | MAY | JUN | JUL | AUG | SEP | OCT | NOV | |
| Swedes | JAN | FEB | MAR | APR | MAY | JUN | JUL | AUG | SEP | OCT | NOV | DEC |
| Sweetcorn | | | | | | | JUL | AUG | SEP | OCT | | |
| Turnips | JAN | FEB | MAR | | MAY | JUN | JUL | AUG | SEP | OCT | NOV | DEC |

## Salads

| | JAN | FEB | MAR | APR | MAY | JUN | JUL | AUG | SEP | OCT | NOV | DEC |
|---|---|---|---|---|---|---|---|---|---|---|---|---|
| Celery | | | | | | JUN | JUL | AUG | SEP | OCT | NOV | DEC |
| Courgettes | | | | | | JUN | JUL | AUG | SEP | OCT | | |
| Cucumbers | | | | APR | MAY | JUN | JUL | AUG | SEP | OCT | | |
| Lettuce (Iceberg) | | | | | MAY | JUN | JUL | AUG | SEP | OCT | | |
| Lettuce (Lollo Rosso) | | | | | MAY | JUN | JUL | AUG | SEP | OCT | | |
| Lettuce (Red Oakleaf) | | | | | MAY | JUN | JUL | AUG | SEP | OCT | | |
| Lettuce (Round) | JAN | FEB | MAR | APR | MAY | JUN | JUL | AUG | SEP | OCT | NOV | DEC |
| Peppers | | | | APR | MAY | JUN | JUL | AUG | SEP | OCT | NOV | |
| Radish | | | | APR | MAY | JUN | JUL | AUG | SEP | OCT | NOV | |
| Scallions | | | | APR | MAY | JUN | JUL | AUG | SEP | OCT | NOV | |

## Herbs

| | JAN | FEB | MAR | APR | MAY | JUN | JUL | AUG | SEP | OCT | NOV | DEC |
|---|---|---|---|---|---|---|---|---|---|---|---|---|
| Basil | | | | APR | MAY | JUN | JUL | AUG | SEP | OCT | NOV | |
| Chives | | | | | MAY | JUN | JUL | AUG | SEP | OCT | NOV | |
| Coriander | | | | | MAY | JUN | JUL | AUG | SEP | OCT | | |
| Dill | | | | | MAY | JUN | JUL | AUG | SEP | OCT | NOV | |
| Fennel | | | | | | JUN | JUL | AUG | SEP | OCT | NOV | |
| Mint | | | MAR | APR | MAY | JUN | JUL | AUG | SEP | OCT | NOV | DEC |
| Parsley | JAN | | | APR | MAY | JUN | JUL | AUG | SEP | OCT | NOV | DEC |
| Sage | JAN | | | APR | MAY | JUN | JUL | AUG | SEP | OCT | NOV | DEC |
| Thyme | JAN | | | APR | MAY | JUN | JUL | AUG | SEP | OCT | NOV | DEC |

## Fruits

| | JAN | FEB | MAR | APR | MAY | JUN | JUL | AUG | SEP | OCT | NOV | DEC |
|---|---|---|---|---|---|---|---|---|---|---|---|---|
| Apples : Cooking | JAN | FEB | MAR | APR | MAY | JUN | JUL | AUG | SEP | OCT | NOV | DEC |
| Apples : Eating | JAN | FEB | MAR | APR | MAY | | | AUG | SEP | OCT | NOV | DEC |
| Blackberries | | | | | | JUN | JUL | AUG | SEP | | | |
| Blackcurrants | | | | | | JUN | | | | | | |
| Blueberries | | | | | | | JUL | AUG | SEP | | | |
| Gooseberries | | | | | | JUN | JUL | AUG | | | | |
| Loganberries | | | | | | | JUL | | | | | |
| Raspberries | | | | | | JUN | JUL | AUG | SEP | OCT | NOV | |
| Strawberries | | | | | MAY | JUN | JUL | AUG | SEP | OCT | NOV | |
| Tayberries | | | | | | | JUL | | | | | |

## Salads

*Chart courtesy of www.bordbia.ie*

# WEEKLY SHOPPING LIST

■ A weekly shopping list and menu planner are invaluable tools. They take a while to do but will save you time and money. They get easier and faster to do the more you use them. I double up on a lot of ingredients. This means that some ingredients may go into more than one dish. It's a great way of saving money and cutting down on food waste. Writing out what you plan to eat for the week will also help you keep an eye on your family's diet, as well help you incorporate more variety.

Do a slow cooker dish on the day you are busiest. Prepare pancake batter mix the night before or cook the pasta and cool down as per the recipe - it will keep in the fridge for three days. You can get little jobs out of the way in advance to make your life easier on busy days.

For example, make the turkey burgers when you have some spare time and pop them in the freezer. They can be cooked under the grill from frozen when needed. All you have to do on the day is whip up a nice side dish. Taking a few minutes to organise your menu planner will save you loads of time throughout the week.

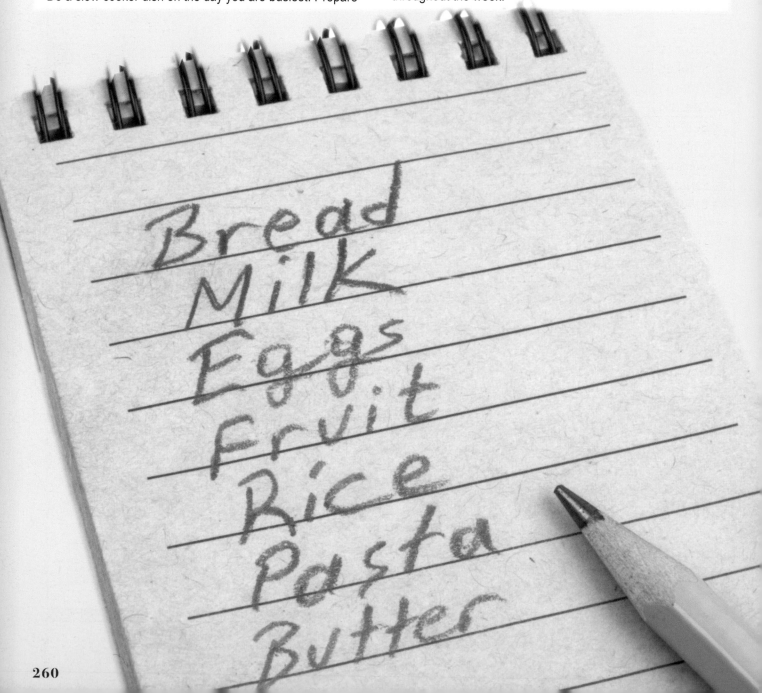

Bread
Milk
Eggs
Fruit
Rice
Pasta
Butter

| Meat | Fish | Dairy | Veggies/Fruit | Dry Goods |
|---|---|---|---|---|
| Chicken breasts (Monday) | Seafood mix (Freeze, defrost Thursday for Friday) | 500g cheddar cheese | Corn on the cob (Frozen, cook from frozen) | Penne Pasta |
| Rib of beef (order and collect Saturday for Sunday) | | Milk | Cauliflower (frozen, cook from frozen) | Rapeseed oil |
| Chicken drumsticks & thighs (Freeze, defrost in fridge Friday night for Saturday) | | 500ml cream | Head of cabbage | Mayonnaise |
| Smoked rashers (Monday & Tuesday) | | Greek yoghurt | Mixed salad leaves | Eggs |
| Beef ribs (order and collect Tuesday for Wednesday) | | Parmesan cheese | Cos lettuce or little gem lettuce | Horseradish |
| Sausages (Tuesday & Wednesday) | | Buttermilk | Garlic | Honey |
| Turkey mince (Freeze, defrost in fridge Wednesday for Thursday) | | Butter | Basil | Spaghetti |
| | | | Mixed peppers, 3 pack | Flour |
| | | | Mushrooms | Bread soda |
| | | | Onions | Salt |
| | | | Frozen berries | Chickpeas (tins) |
| | | | Carrots | Mustard seeds |
| | | | Turnip | Lasagne sheets |
| | | | Parsnip | Tomato ketchup |
| | | | Rosemary | Brown sauce |
| | | | Lemon | Worcestershire sauce |
| | | | Courgettes | Oyster sauce |
| | | | Sweet potatoes | Sweet chilli |
| | | | Rooster potatoes | Salt |
| | | | Tomatoes | Stock Cubes |
| | | | Cherry tomatoes | Burger buns/baps |
| | | | Thyme | Olive oil |